W9-CZU-308

THE POLITICS OF LINGUISTICS

THE POLITICS OF
LINGUISTICS

FREDERICK J. NEWMEYER

THE UNIVERSITY OF
CHICAGO PRESS

155807

Published by arrangement with Pantheon Books,
A Division of Random House, Inc.

THE UNIVERSITY OF CHICAGO PRESS, CHICAGO 60637

© 1986 by Frederick J. Newmeyer
All rights reserved. Published 1986
Printed in the United States of America

95 94 93 92 91 90 89 88 87 86   5 4 3 2 1

FREDERICK J. NEWMEYER has written extensively about formal
grammatical analysis, linguistic theory, and the history of linguistics. He is professor of linguistics at the University of Washington, Seattle, and has taught at the University of London,
Cornell University, Wayne State University, and the University of
California, Los Angeles. He has also been an associate editor of the
journal *Language,* and the *Journal of Pragmatics.*

LIBRARY OF CONGRESS CATALOGING-IN-PUBLICATION DATA

Newmeyer, Frederick J.
   The politics of linguistics.

   Bibliography: p.
   Includes index.
   1. Linguistics—History—19th century.
   2. Linguistics—History—20th century. I. Title.
   P93.N48 1986   410'.9   86-11225
   ISBN 0-226-57720-1

CONTENTS

v

155807

ACKNOWLEDGMENTS

M Y GREATEST debt is to those who read through the prefinal manuscript and provided me with helpful suggestions: Sandra Silberstein, Evan Watkins, Joseph Emonds, Alan Nasser, Ellen Kaisse, Sol Saporta, and Keith Percival. It goes without saying that none of these individuals is responsible for errors of either fact or interpretation. No doubt I shall soon regret not heeding more of their advice.

So many persons provided me with information and advice that I am not sure that I can remember them all. The following stand out in my mind as being particularly worthy of acknowledgment: Dwight Bolinger, William Bright, Noam Chomsky, Michael Covington, Edward Finegan, John Fought, John Goldsmith, Kenneth Hale, Morris Halle, John Hammer, Eric Hamp, Victor Hanzeli, Fred Householder, Jay Keyser, Paul Kiparsky, William Labov, Peter Ladefoged, Geoffrey Nunberg, David Pesetsky, Kenneth Pike, Geoffrey Pullum, R. H. Robins, Carlota Smith, Robert Stockwell, and Ladislaw Zgusta.

1

THE STUDY OF LANGUAGE

THE ability to speak is the most characteristically human of all human attributes. Philosophers since the ancient Greeks have pointed to language as the most significant feature that separates us from the beasts. So great is the disparity between speech and any form of animal communication that it remains the most difficult human trait for which to provide an evolutionary account. Not even our closest primate relatives have anything like it.[1] Moreover, the uniqueness of language is matched by its pervasiveness. There is hardly a significant facet of our lives in which it does not play a role. We communicate primarily by means of language, we think

3

and reason in it, and in creative expression we tailor it to our imagination. Our sleeping hours are no less free from language than our waking ones — language is even a medium in which our dreams are conveyed. Little wonder that literary critics, philosophers, and developmental psychologists alike have taken the analysis of language as their starting point, and that the computer industry regards the construction of a program that models human language to be its most important goal for the next decade.

A sign of the pervasiveness of language is that there are as many different approaches to its study as there are to knowledge in general. The humanist, the social scientist, and the natural scientist each has a stake in understanding how language works; each branch of scholarship approaches language with its particular set of assumptions and methodologies, and focuses on that aspect most germane to its central concerns. A humanist, for example, might investigate the role language plays in the process of literary creativity or as a medium through which values are formed and expressed. In this view, language is a mirror of our cultural heritage, our link with the past, the embodiment of all that is both human and noble. And thus to study its nature is to probe the very essence of the human spirit. For many, humanistic concerns provide the best — or even the only — motivation for analyzing language; as the literary critic Ian Robinson puts it, "Language is a fitting object of study because there are things like *King Lear*."[2]

The humanistic study of language has been established for well over two millennia. The Greeks, for example, hoped that linguistic investigations would lead to a better understanding of the language of the Homeric epics, and even more generally to a solution of critical philosophical questions. The fact that Aristotle's sketch of Greek grammar appears in his *Poetics* reflects the humanistic goals that motivated his linguistic research. Such goals have remained central to language study; even today, a greater volume of research is devoted to creative expression in language than any other linguistic topic.

Others approach language from a sociological vantage point. Language is, after all, the most characteristic medium of social exchange; it must therefore both reflect and influence all facets of our social existence. The appeal of studying language in its social context is the promise that doing so might offer a key to an understanding of society itself. From this perspective, the self-evidently social nature of language is the obvious starting point for linguistic research. Anyone whose goal is an understanding of human interaction must take an interest in how speakers use language to inform, to deceive, to convince, to express hostility or group solidarity, and so on. Concern with the social context of speech is by no means purely academic; many pressing political issues revolve around language, from the question of the relative status that should be granted to the indigenous and colonial languages in newly independent Third World nations to the question of whether Chicano children in American cities have the right to an education in Spanish.

Still others approach language as a natural scientist would study a physical phenomenon, that is, by focusing on those of its properties that exist apart from either the beliefs and values of the individual speakers of a language or the nature of the society in which the language is spoken. Work in "autonomous linguistics," as we might call it, ranges from simple accounts of changes in pronunciation and descriptive statements ("grammars") of the structural regularities in particular languages to ambitious attempts to characterize universal limits within which languages may differ structurally.

While all autonomous linguists share the belief that a language can be analyzed successfully without taking into consideration the society or beliefs of its speakers, some find the puzzle-solving nature of grammar construction an intellectually satisfying end in itself, and explicitly reject any possible broader implications of such an enterprise. Others, however, believe that an understanding of grammatical structure is relevant to an understanding of other structured human attributes, including the mind itself. Indeed, since its inception in the early nineteenth century, the great appeal of the autonomous approach to linguistics has been a widespread feeling that the systematicity of its subject matter—the unconscious and nonsocietally determined component of language—has implications that go well beyond the field of linguistics. For example, the discovery by autonomous linguists in the past century that languages had undergone the same sorts of systematic changes throughout history profoundly impressed contemporary evolutionary thinkers such as Darwin, Lyell, Marx, and Engels; they saw language as an important model of a human attribute whose development seemed to be guided by a uniform set of principles. Furthermore, the fact that linguistic changes were, by and large, not subject to conscious awareness influenced and encouraged contemporary psychologists, who were just beginning to appreciate the importance of the unconscious in human mental functioning.

The degree of success attained by twentieth-century autonomous linguists in characterizing the structural regularities of language has been the envy of many social scientists, who have attempted to find analogous regularities within their own areas of inquiry. Autonomous linguistics seems to bridge the natural sciences and the human sciences, to combine a thoroughly human subject matter with a precision and depth matched only in the hard sciences. In the words of one enthusiastic commentator: "What mathematics already is for the physical sciences, [autonomous] linguistics can be for the social sciences."[3]

In the past quarter century, both the scope and prestige of autonomous linguistics have increased even more as we have come to understand the connection between the structure of language and the structure of mind. Noam Chomsky of the Massachusetts Institute of Technology has developed the position that all humans are endowed with an innate and highly structured predisposition toward language; the grammar described by the linguist is thus literally "in the head" of the speaker. The discovery of the biological nature of human linguistic uniqueness has had implications that stretch well beyond the field of linguistics; indeed, the discovery has sparked an interdisciplinary research program that includes philosophers, who see in Chomsky's theory a way of reconstituting classical rationalism along modern lines; psychologists, who study the nature and development of abstract grammatical structures and their relationship to other cognitive faculties; neurologists, who investigate

7

the physical embodiment of these structures; and language teachers, who derive from this approach a method of teaching that draws more directly on the learner's internalized grammatical knowledge than the traditional hear-and-repeat method.

The field of linguistics, most broadly conceived, represents these three orientations — humanistic, sociological, and autonomous. The interests of humanistic linguists are embodied in the related subfields of "poetics" and "stylistics," which are devoted to the linguistic analysis of literary texts and to the study of the figurative, aesthetic, and creative use of language in literature. The functioning of language in society is the province of "sociolinguistics," which addresses such topics as language variation, the ethnography of speaking, and national language planning, among others. "Pragmatics" and "discourse analysis," two other sociologically oriented aspects of language study, describe language use in its interpersonal context. A typical paper in pragmatics might describe the various linguistic devices a speaker has available for making indirect requests (for example, by saying "Could you pass the salt?" or "I would like the salt" or "Is there any salt?" instead of "Please pass the salt"), while discourse analysts concern themselves with such questions as the conventions governing turn-taking in conversation. Most work in autonomous linguistics falls under the heading of "grammatical theory."* This branch of linguistics attempts to formulate the principles governing structural regularity in language. Its principal

---

* Autonomous linguistics also includes work in the field of "phonetics," which studies the physical and articulatory properties of speech sounds.

subareas are "phonology," the study of sound patterning; "morphology," the study of word formation; and "syntax," the study of sentence construction.

Not every branch of linguistics can neatly be characterized as "humanistic," "sociological," or "autonomous." Work in "semantics," the study of meaning, encompasses all three orientations, as does "historical linguistics," the study of language change. And "psycholinguistics," which addresses itself to such topics as children's acquisition of language and the principles governing speech perception and production, can be approached from either a sociological or a grammatical direction. However, individual semanticists, historical linguists, or psycholinguists, who take more than one approach to their subject matter are quite rare.

Interestingly, the *profession* of linguistics—that is, the body of scholars who at any particular time and place are regarded as "linguists"—has always been far more restrictive in its self-definition than what one might assume given the wide-ranging interests of the field. For example, in the United States today, the humanistic approach to the study of language is not even generally regarded as falling under the rubric of "linguistics," and those who practice it are almost always found in literature rather than linguistics departments. The lack of interest with which American linguists tend to regard such areas as stylistics and poetics can be appreciated by an examination of the most popular introductory linguistics text— Fromkin and Rodman's *An Introduction to Language.*[4] Discussion of the methods and results of grammatical theory makes up about eighty percent of the material in the book, and that pertaining to language in society about twenty percent. There is not a word about language in literature or about its aesthetic properties.

In other countries, the profession is very different. In Europe, it is taken for granted that the humanistic study of language is part of linguistics. In most European countries with the exception of Great Britain and the Netherlands, the sociological and humanistic orientations predominate, and autonomous linguists make up a rather small percentage of the profession. Even in long-time centers of grammatical study like Prague, Geneva, and Copenhagen, autonomous linguistics is overshadowed by other orientations.

While some notable figures in linguistics, such as the American Edward Sapir and the Russian Roman Jakobson, have combined the different approaches to language in their work, the pervasive tendency in the field has been to insist that language can be studied in one way only. In fact, the term "linguistics" has continually been redefined to exclude whichever approaches happen to be out of favor. Around the turn of the century, for example, the Italian idealist philosopher Benedetto Croce equated linguistics with aesthetics, heaping scorn on those who would study primarily the grammatical or social aspects of language.[5] More recently, the American linguist William Labov disputed the definition of sociolinguistics as "something apart from linguistics," insisting that even the grammatical aspects of language, upon close inspection, will reveal their fundamentally sociological nature.[6] At the other extreme, many grammarians have defined the field solely in terms of the goals of autonomous linguistics. For example, in one introduction to English syntax, the goal of the linguist is defined as: "to arrive at a statement of the rules that form the basis of a person's ability to speak and comprehend a particular language, and, by the study of many languages and of the human organism itself, to arrive at a statement of the rules of universal grammar."[7]

These restrictive redefinitions of the field have frequently been accompanied by a denigration of the basic intellectual worth of the competing orientations. Members of both the humanistic and sociological schools reject autonomous linguistics — which focuses on isolated grammatical rules — for failing to shed light on language as it is *actually used:* in everyday communication, in creative expression, or to support or challenge the dominant social ideology. M. A. K. Halliday, for example, has accused autonomous linguists of "[excluding] social context from the study of language," and George Lakoff concurs, charging that autonomous linguists "set up artificial boundaries and rule out of the study of language such things as human reasoning, context, social interaction, deixis, fuzziness, sarcasm, discourse types, fragments, variation among speakers, etc."[8]

The opposition to autonomous linguistics frequently expresses its disagreement in explicitly political terms. Thus, the American sociolinguist Dell Hymes maintains that the notion of autonomous grammatical structures is an "ideological" one, which implies the existence of "an abstract and isolated individual, not, except contingently, of a person in a social world."[9] European Marxists have typically taken the position that only an "idealist" could consider abstracting any aspect of language from its social context; a materialist approach to language must begin by rejecting such an abstraction.[10]

Chomsky, as the leading exponent of autonomous linguistics in the world today, is particularly singled out for attack. The debate over his ideas has, by any criteria, frequently exceeded the normal bounds of partisan scholarship. One critic recently asserted that Chomsky's theories "can only be described as Fascist in character." Another denounced his supporters for "worm[ing] their way into power in a number of linguistics departments" by using a technique that was "exactly the same as that of the Fascists and Communists in seizing political power."[11]

Autonomous linguists, for their part, have traditionally maintained that theirs is the only *scientific* approach to language. Consequently, they have tended to dismiss the work of sociolinguists as little more than a hodgepodge of anecdotes and spurious statistical correlations, all but devoid of intellectual content. Chomsky's view is typical: he considers even "the existence of a discipline called 'sociolinguistics' . . . an obscure matter,"[12] an attitude that reflects his opinion of the social sciences in general. In sociology, Chomsky told an interviewer,

> one finds observations, intuitions, impressions, some valid generalizations perhaps. All very valuable, no doubt, but not at the level of explanatory principles. . . . Sociolinguistics is . . . a discipline that seeks to apply principles of sociology to the study of language; but I suspect that it can draw little from sociology, and I wonder whether it is likely to contribute much to it. . . . You can also collect butterflies and make many observations. If you like butterflies, that's fine; but such work must not be confused with research, which is concerned to dis-

cover explanatory principles of some depth and fails
if it does not do so.[13]

Linguistics is certainly not unique in the fact that its
subject matter can be approached from a variety of direc-
tions. Fields as diverse as philosophy, psychology, and
history lend themselves to both humanistic and sociological orientations, one or the other of which has
been the more prominent at different stages of the field's
development. Moreover the "quantitative methods" currently popular in the social sciences represent, in a certain sense, an "autonomous" approach, since such
methods are characteristically neither derived from nor
applied to any general theory of society. But linguistics is
remarkable among other disciplines for the prominence
the autonomous orientation has achieved over the last
century, and the vehemence with which it is challenged.
Indeed, the debates over autonomy have time and again
been carried on with a fervor more characteristic of the
political arena than of academia.

But what accounts for the success of autonomous linguistics and the passionate opposition to it? Clearly, autonomous linguistics has been able to offer a set of solutions to complex linguistic problems, but one can hardly
expect, particularly in the human sciences, that a "correct" approach (whatever that might mean in fact) will
necessarily be accepted. Indeed, the success of autonomous linguistics results to a considerable degree from the
fact that powerful institutions have found it expedient to
support it. And the fortunes of the opposition to autonomous linguistics have equally been linked with external
political factors. In certain places and in certain historical
periods, both the humanistic and the sociological orienta-

tions to language have found themselves explicitly championed by particular ideologies. Consequently, debates within linguistics have often mirrored debates within the larger society, giving the field a highly politicized character.

While the development of the humanistic or sociological schools will not be treated here in nearly the same detail as the autonomous, this should not be taken to reflect a negative personal evaluation of either their importance or their intrinsic interest. The focus on autonomous linguistics in these pages results from the fact that the ideological controversies surrounding it play on a number of themes central to modern intellectual history while at the same time bringing out the salient features of the two alternative orientations. Hence the discussion of the latter will be devoted largely, though not exclusively, to the objections their practitioners have raised to the theories and practice of autonomous linguistics.

Just as its subject matter has endowed the field of linguistics with an importance far out of proportion to the number of practicing linguists, so too have its debates engendered an interest from the outside well beyond what one might expect. The leading intellectual figures of the past two centuries and, at certain times, even national governments have monitored the progress of the field and the conflicts within it. We too, in the following pages, will focus our attention on the development of the field, on its successes, and on its internal strife. And we will come to understand why the impressive results of the past two centuries have so often been overshadowed by bitter conflict—conflict that is far from being resolved.

2

THE RISE OF

AUTONOMOUS LINGUISTICS

M ODERN linguistics dates from the end of the eighteenth century. In 1786 the British "orientalist" Sir William Jones, of the East India Company, read his famous paper to the Royal Asiatic Society in Calcutta in which he suggested the kinship and common origin of the Sanskrit language once spoken in India and several European languages. In Jones's words:

The Sanskrit language, whatever may be its antiquity, is of a wonderful structure; more perfect than the Greek, more copious than the Latin, and more exquisitely refined than either; yet bearing to both of them a stronger affinity, both in the roots of verbs and in the forms of grammar, than could have been produced by accident; so strong that no philologer could examine the Sanskrit, Greek, and Latin, without believing them to have sprung from some common source, which, perhaps, no longer exists. There is a similar reason, though not quite so forcible, for supposing that both the Gothic and the Celtic had the same origin with the Sanskrit.[1]

Jones's statement led to one of the great intellectual achievements of the nineteenth century—the methods and results of the field of comparative linguistics.* Comparativists were not only able to verify Jones's speculation, but also succeeded in showing that most of the languages spoken in Europe, India, and Iran belonged to the same family. Further application of the "comparative method" (as it is called) resulted in the hypothesis that the four-thousand-odd languages of the world belong to several dozen families at most. In broadest outline, two languages are considered to be in the same family if they are descended from the same ancestor, or "protolanguage." Comparativists look for systematic correspondences in sound and meaning among the languages under investigation. If enough are found that are not attributable to borrowing from one language to another, it is hypothesized that the languages are genetically related, i.e., that they belong to the same family. Since most of the time no written records of the protolanguage exist,

---

* The field has also been known at various times as "historical and comparative linguistics," "historical linguistics," and "comparative philology." I will refer to its practitioners as "comparativists" throughout this work.

18

a major task of comparative linguistics has been to reconstruct a protolanguage for each language family and to formulate the sound changes by which it descended into its various daughter tongues.

Probably the best-known result of comparative linguistics was formulated early in the nineteenth century by Jacob Grimm (1785–1863) and hence came to be known as "Grimm's Law." Grimm observed regular correspondences between sounds in the Germanic languages (English, German, and the Scandinavian tongues, among others) and in many other languages of Europe and India. For example, where Germanic has an *f*, the others characteristically have a *p* (English *father*, Greek *patēr*; English *fish*, Latin *piscis*); Germanic *th* corresponds to *t* in the other languages (English *three*, Sanskrit *trayaḥ*; English *thou*, Lithuanian *tù*); and so on. This observation was the first link in a chain of reasoning that led to the hypothesis that a disdnct Germanic protolanguage literally came into being as a result of a systematic shift of sounds in one part of the ancestral speech community. It further led to the reconstruction of the presumed protolanguage, "Proto-Indo-European," from which Germanic and many of the other languages of Europe and India descended.

While the methods of comparative linguistics came ultimately to represent the autonomous orientation to language par excellence, the earliest comparativists certainly did not feel that they were looking at language as an "autonomous" entity. Comparative linguistics was born during the romantic movement that swept Europe at the end of the eighteenth century. Romanticists, in opposition to the Enlightenment rationalists who preceded them, believed that it was fruitless to attempt to study human beings in isolation from their surrounding world, which, moreover, could not be understood without recourse to the past that shaped it. Hence romantics began to look beyond Europe to record the customs, religions, and languages of the ancient peoples of the East. And they turned their attention to native and national customs and beliefs, to folklore, and to local forms of speech, no matter how "barbarous" these may have seemed to a previous generation of scholars. In short, the comparative studies that launched modern linguistics were perfectly in tune with romantic goals.* Thus, Grimm, who with his brother collected the famous fairy tales, considered the preservation of folk beliefs and the formulation of Germanic sound changes analogous — for him both represented the search for one's roots in the past and the key to a better understanding of the present. For example, Grimm believed that the consonant change expressed the very qualities that distinguish the German people. He rhapsodized:

> From one point of view the sound shift seems to me to be a barbarous aberration from which other quieter nations refrained, but which has to do with the violent progress and yearning for liberty as found in Germany in the early Middle Ages, and which started the transformation of Europe.[2]

* As many commentators have observed, the romantic movement (and, by extension, comparative linguistics) originated in part as a result of the increased awareness of non-Western cultures that resulted from European colonial expansion. For example, the "discovery" of Sanskrit was a by-product of the British conquest of India.

Nevertheless, as it progressed in the course of the nineteenth century, the actual practice of comparative linguistics became increasingly divorced from the romanticist program. The comparativists of the first half of the century, in keeping with contemporary romantic sentiment, believed that their work would lead them inexorably toward the discovery of the one pristine uncorrupted language common to all humanity. But as that hope receded, two other ideas emerged. First, it became apparent that the method they were developing was a general one: it was every bit as applicable to sound changes taking place in contemporary urbanized Europe as to those in dim prehistory. For example, the comparative method could be applied to the modern Romance languages in the reconstruction of Proto-Romance (i.e., spoken Latin) with the same degree of success as to the classical languages in the reconstruction of Proto-Indo-European. Moreover, they found that the principles of the comparative method functioned independently of the culture, society, beliefs, or personalities of the speakers of the languages treated. Indeed, such "anthropological" facts played no role at all in the historical reconstruction of a protolanguage. The only basis necessary for the successful application of the method was a systematic comparison of sound and meaning correspondences between related languages or dialects. In short, it became accepted among comparativists, first in their practice alone, and then in their theoretical pronouncements as well, that comparative linguistics was an autonomous discipline.

The development of comparative linguistics touched on every significant intellectual movement of the century. From the very beginning, it came into conflict with the more traditional approaches to the study of language history. In particular, its methods and conclusions rankled many students of classical philology—those whose principal interest in languages such as classical Greek and Latin was not derived from a desire to understand language change in general, but rather from the hope that an investigation of the literary texts in those languages would grant a better appreciation of the cultures of antiquity. Many classical philologists looked with resentment and scorn on the comparativists, both for their intellectually unsettling interest in languages that had no literary tradition, and for their greater interest in the formal features of classical languages than in the content of their literature.*

But whereas the classical philologists spoke from a humanist perspective, comparative linguists regarded themselves as having a "scientific" approach to language. Along with their fellow romantics, they rejected

* The differences between the classical philologists and the comparativists were often reflected in differences in political orientation as well. Many (though by no means all) of the former lent their support to the authoritarian old regimes, and resisted the wave of revolt that was sweeping Europe at the time. While Versailles or Hampton Court might not equal the grandeur of ancient Greece or Rome, the classical philologists certainly felt more affinity for such splendors than they ever could for the hut of a Lithuanian peasant. The comparativists, on the other hand, identified for the most part with radical political movements. Sir William Jones, for example, was forced to withdraw from the parliamentary election of 1780 due to his opposition to the American War and to the slave trade.[3] Jacob Grimm was dismissed from his position at the University of Göttingen in 1837 for protesting against the king of Hanover's abrogation of the constitution. And Wilhelm von Humboldt, who produced an important early descriptive study of a non-Indo-European language (the Kawi language of Java), has been described as "the most prominent representative in Germany of the doctrine of natural rights and of the opposition to the authoritarian state."[4]

the earlier rationalist view of science that had championed Newtonian physics as a model and had thus seen nature as a gigantic machine. The romantics also had a scientific model, but they took their inspiration from biology. The popular metaphor of the time was the "organism," a totality that regulated and coordinated its component parts—unlike the Newtonian machine, which was merely the sum of its parts. But the romanticist view extended beyond "metaphor"; many early comparative linguists believed that language was literally an organism.

As the German comparativist Franz Bopp wrote in 1827:

> Languages must be regarded as organic bodies, formed in accordance with definite laws; bearing within themselves an internal principle of life, they develop and they gradually die out, after, no longer comprehending themselves, they discard, mutilate or misuse . . . components or forms which were originally significant but which have gradually become relatively superficial appendages.[5]

And his contemporary August Pott sounded the same theme:

> A language is in a constant state of change throughout its life: like every organic object, it has periods of gestation and maturation, times of accelerated and of slackened growth, its prime, decay, and gradual extinction.[6]

August Schleicher (1821–1868), one of the century's most outstanding comparativists, pushed the organism theory to its limits, hypothesizing that typological differences among languages represent different stages of evolutionary development, which themselves correspond to the three levels of development of the natural world: crystals, plants, and animals.

Paradoxically, the view of languages as organic provided the early comparativists with the perfect vehicle for the expression of autonomy. While they recognized, of course, that languages, like plants and animals, were affected by their environment to one degree or another, they also believed that every organism possessed a (never fully explicated) "internal principle of life" that determined its development and structural characteristics. Since each plant, animal, and language had its own immutable internal principle, each such organism was, in effect, "autonomous" with respect to all of the others. Just as the early nineteenth-century evolutionary biologists believed that plants and animals were predestined to evolve in a particular manner, so too their contemporaries in linguistics believed that the tendency to undergo particular sound changes was inherent in the languages themselves.

By the 1870s, however, virtually all linguists had abandoned the idea that languages could profitably be regarded as organisms. The crucial blow to such an idea was the general acceptance within scientific circles of the Darwinian model of evolution. If at this point comparativists had wished to uphold the organismic theory, they would have been forced to interpret language change according to the principles of natural selection. But to most comparativists, it had become clear that the internal characteristics of a particular language had little if anything to do with its chances for survival. By the final quarter of the century, the notion of autonomy had parted ways with the view of language as an "organism," a move which reflected the growing recognition of the distinctive aspects of the discipline of linguistics.

The methods and results of comparative linguistics had been an inspiration for thinkers in many other fields. After all, linguists had taken an evolutionary approach to their subject matter early in the century, long before Darwinian evolutionary thinking had become fashionable. The pioneering role that linguists had played was freely acknowledged by the leading figures of the period — Darwin in biology, Lyell in geology, Marx and Engels in history, Spencer in sociology — who referred in admiring tones to the results of the field. Both Darwin and Lyell, for example, cited work in comparative linguistics, which they saw as providing a model of the evolutionary process, and social scientists as well looked to comparative linguistics for inspiration. It was reasoned that since it is possible to reconstruct an ancestral language through the systematic comparison of the forms present in its descendant tongues, it should be possible to reconstruct ancestral forms of mythology, religion, law, and so on by comparing such institutions in *cultures* springing from a common source. So, for example, Sir Henry Maine attempted to reconstruct via the comparative method the original legal institutions of the Indo-European peoples. In his *Village Communities in the East and West* (1872), he stated explicitly that he was constructing a comparative jurisprudence on the model of comparative linguistics.

However, Maine himself remarked on the limitations of his undertaking:

I should, however, be making very idle pretension if I held a prospect of obtaining, by the application of the Comparative Method to jurisprudence, any results which in point of interest or trustworthiness are to be placed on a level with those which, for example, have been accomplished in Comparative Philology. To give only one reason, the phenomena of human society, laws and legal ideas, opinions and usages are vastly more affected by external circumstances than language. They are more at the mercy of individual volition and consequently much more subject to change effected deliberately from without.[7]

In other words, Maine believed with the linguists that the success of the comparative method in linguistics was a function of the autonomy of linguistic form and that no analogue to autonomy appeared to exist in jurisprudence, which, like other social institutions "are vastly more affected by external circumstances than language."

This privileged "autonomy" of language was bound to affect the emphasis of linguistic studies in many areas. In particular, it led linguists to explore the possibility that aspects of language other than the diachronic (i.e., historical) could profitably be studied as an autonomous entity. It is hardly surprising that theorizing about language in the nineteenth century had been, for the most part, diachronically oriented, since historicism, as we have seen, dominated most fields of inquiry. One prominent comparativist of the time even went so far as to deny the possibility that anything nonhistorical in language could be treated scientifically.[8] Even so, synchronic grammatical studies, that is, those covering one particular language at one point in time, were published by the hundreds in the nineteenth century. But with rare exception, those who saw themselves as *linguists* did not consider the writing of such grammars as an important task; it was the less interesting, less scientific enterprise which could be left to the more traditionally oriented philologists, to the pedagogues, and to the missionaries.

But even before the century had ended, the rigid equation of the historical with the scientific had begun to erode. The first steps toward a theory of synchronic linguistics were taken almost simultaneously by a dozen different linguists in as many countries. Most of these theorists of language synchrony need no mention outside of a historiography of linguistics. However, the thinking of one individual — Ferdinand de Saussure (1857–1913) — looms so large in the history of the field and has had such a profound influence on the development of so many disciplines that he has come to be considered one of the intellectual giants of modern times. Saussure's lecture notes, published posthumously in 1916 as the *Cours de Linguistique Générale*, laid out the basic tenets of structural linguistics, which, in its various forms, was to become the leading approach to linguistic analysis in the twentieth century. The fundamental tenet of the *Cours* is that synchronic aspects of language — such as its principles of sound patterning and word formation — as well as diachronic can be studied productively as an autonomous entity. In the final sentence of the book, we find the classic statement of the autonomy

155807

of synchronic linguistics: "*The true and unique object of linguistics is language studied in and for itself.*"[9] The linguists of this century have largely been engaged in developing the ideas implicit in this statement, or in attempting to show that they are fundamentally misguided.

3

STRUCTURAL LINGUISTICS

A T THE time of his death in 1913, the idea that Saussure would come to be regarded as the pioneering figure of twentieth-century synchronic linguistics would have generated laughter, had anybody even considered raising it. Virtually all of his writings dealt with diachrony (he made important contributions to Indo-European comparative linguistics), and only in the last few years of his life did he begin lecturing on synchrony at all. But soon after he died, two of his colleagues at the University of Geneva edited for publication the notes that his students had taken at these lectures. While the resultant *Cours de Linguistique Générale* attracted little immediate attention, a quarter century later many of the world's most prominent linguists had come to regard it as their main source of inspiration. Saussure's reputation has not been dimmed even by the discovery in the 1950s that the *Cours* diverges in serious ways both from his own lecture notes and from those students' notes on which it was based. The myth is now greater than the man, and, not surprisingly, a mini-industry has flourished devoted to sorting out what Saussure "really believed."

The central principle of the *Cours* is that the systematicity of language is confined to a well-defined subpart, which can be abstracted from the totality of speech. This subpart Saussure called "*langue*," which he contrasted with "*parole*," or "speech." *Langue* represents the abstract system of structural relationships inherent in language, relationships that are held in common by all members of a speech community. *Parole*, on the other hand, represents the individual act of speaking, which is never performed exactly the same way twice. Saussure compared language to a symphony. *Langue* represents the unvarying score, *parole* the actual performance, no two of which are alike. Since, in the Saussurian view, *langue* forms a coherent structural system, any approach to language devoted to explicating the internal workings of this system has come to be known as "structural linguistics" or simply as "structuralism."

All varieties of structural linguistics approach the language under analysis on its own terms, as a discrete object of investigation. As a result, the principles governing *langue* emerge with their own internal dynamic; they are not reflections of principles developed by other fields of inquiry, such as sociology, psychology, physiology, or whatever. In this sense, the product of a structural analysis—a grammar—is an autonomous entity, and structural linguistics is thus an autonomous discipline.[1]

Models of *langue* typically consist of three components: the *phonology*, which deals with principles of sound combination; the *morphology*, which deals with principles of word formation; and the *syntax*, which deals with relationships between words and larger constructions in the language. Let us consider some concrete examples. In English, the "p" sound, when it occurs at the beginning of a word, is always produced with accompanying aspiration (a puff of breath), whereas there is no aspiration if the "p" follows an "s" (contrast *pin* and *spin*, *pool* and *spool*, etc.). Such a generalization is stated in the phonology, where the sounds that comprise the "p" "phoneme" (sound class) are listed, along with the positions in the word in which they can occur. A morphological generalization about English is that the prefix *un-* and the suffix *-able* are both units of word formation, or "morphemes." The word *unbreakable*, for example, in a structuralist analysis consists of the three morphemes *un-*, *-break-*, and *-able*. The syntax of English in a structuralist grammar minimally contains information about the syntactic category ("part of speech") to which a word belongs. For example, it will assign the words *may, will,* and *can* to a category, Modal Auxiliary, distinct from the category, Verb, that contains *run, know, eat,* etc., since the former, unlike the latter, never take inflectional endings. But different structuralist frameworks disagree over the question of how much syntax can be subsumed under *langue*. Virtually all have attributed to *langue* categorical information such as that just described. But fewer have attempted to deal with the grouping of sequences of words into larger phrases (e.g., with whatever might determine that the major break in the sentence *the old man came to town* is between *man* and *came,* not between *old* and *man*). And fewer still have opted for a structural treatment of the similarities and differences between sentences (e.g., with the precise characterization of the differences in structure between an active transitive sentence like *John threw the ball* and its passive counterpart *the ball was thrown by John*). Most structuralists (until, at least, quite recently) have taken the view that the latter two types of syntactic phenomena have been too unsystematic and idiosyncratic to be suitable for structural treatment within *langue.*

A structuralist description of a language typically takes the form of an inventory of the phonemes, morphemes, and syntactic categories of the language under analysis, along with a statement of the positions in which these elements occur. The point of such a taxonomy of *langue* was made explicit in the *Cours:*

> It would be interesting from a practical viewpoint to begin with units, to determine what they are and to account for their diversity by classifying them. . . . Next we would have to classify the subunits, then the larger units, etc. By determining in this way the elements that it manipulates, synchronic linguistics would completely fulfill its task, for it would relate all synchronic phenomena to their fundamental principle.[2]

The idea that language might contain an isolable core of discrete units standing in systematic interrelationship with each other captured the imaginations of the world's linguists. While earlier synchronic accounts of language had often been rich in observations about the various grammatical processes at work in the language under discussion, they had never approached the language as a whole as a coherent system. Structural linguistics endowed the field with a rich research program whose goal was to make precise the nature of such systems.

By the late 1930s, structural linguistics was flourishing in a variety of Western academic centers—in particular, Prague, Copenhagen, Paris, Geneva, London, Chicago, and New Haven. The most active and successful center was Prague, where structuralist phonology was developed to a high degree of sophistication. In a sense, the Prague School had a head start; one of its leading figures, Roman Jakobson, had played an important role in the prerevolutionary formalist movement in Russia. Russian formalism, which advocated treating works of art and literature independently of their social context, helped lead Jakobson to the view that language, too, could be treated as a structural object of autonomous analysis.

By the 1940s, the significance of developments in structural linguistics had become apparent even outside the field. If one branch of the human sciences could uncover invariant basic units, many reasoned, then why not others as well? Perhaps every sphere of human experience was organized in an analogous plan of order and rationality. Scholars in a number of disciplines began to search for the equivalents of *langue* and *parole* within their own fields.

In America, the impact of structural linguistics was felt first and most strongly in anthropology. A. L. Kroeber's question, "What is the cultural equivalent of the phoneme?"[3] sparked a decade of anthropological research devoted to pushing the linguistic analogy to its limits. By the end of the 1950s, Clyde Kluckhohn could write that "the distinctive aspects of the anthropological outlook derive primarily from the [fact that] among behavioral scientists, only cultural anthropologists have been in sustained contact with the extraordinary developments in structural linguistics over the past generation."[4] The influence of structural linguistics in the United States soon extended to other spheres of inquiry, ranging from social psychology to the analysis of the language used in political tracts to literary criticism.[5]

The basic concepts of structural linguistics had even greater repercussions on scholarship in Europe, particularly in France. During the Second World War, Roman Jakobson and the French anthropologist Claude Lévi-Strauss found themselves in exile together in New York, the former teaching at the French "university in exile," the École Libre des Hautes Études, the latter at the New School for Social Research. Their discussions led Lévi-Strauss to formulate the ideas of structural anthropology, an approach to the analysis of culture for which Lévi-Strauss never failed to credit Jakobson and Saussure. Indeed, Lévi-Strauss compared the linguists' discovery of structurally patterned phonemes and morphemes to the Newtonian revolution in physics.[6] By the 1960s, Lévi-Strauss's work had triggered a major intellectual movement in France, represented by such figures as Roland Barthes in literature, Michael Foucault in history, Jacques Lacan in psychoanalysis, and Louis Althusser in Marxism.

Ironically, the intellectual trends generated by structural linguistics have enjoyed more success in postwar Europe than structural linguistics itself. Despite its roots there, structural linguistics lost momentum in continental Europe in the 1940s and 1950s. European structuralists, outside of Czechoslovakia, were in general unable to develop either the organizational autonomy within academia or the sense of common professional purpose necessary to succeed as a movement. Moreover, what the Prague School had built in Czechoslovakia was quickly destroyed by the war, which sent many of its leading members, like Jakobson, into exile, and by the postwar regime, which officially ended its activities.

The political opposition to structural linguistics was strong enough to keep it from gaining a foothold in other places as well. Both Nazi Germany and fascist Italy had officially condemned structuralism as incompatible with the ideology of the state. During the Nazi period, the pages of German linguistic journals were filled with vivid descriptions of how the German soul manifests itself in its people's masterful language. Likewise, in Italy in this era, many accounts of language consisted of a peculiar mixture of aesthetics and nation-worship, as scholars strove at one and the same time to identify the features of a particular language with the presumed spiritual characteristics of its speakers and to demonstrate the superiority of Italian as a medium of creative expression. The state sponsorship of such an approach to linguistic matters naturally went along with official disapproval of structural linguistics. Indeed, practically no structural linguistics was done at all in Germany and Italy in this period. Structuralism, with its value-free analysis of individual languages and equal attention to all of them, regardless of the race or cultural level of their speakers, was anathema to official ideology in those countries.

At the same time that structural linguistics was condemned for its egalitarian outlook in Germany and Italy, in the Soviet Union before 1950 it was outlawed for being a product of bourgeois ideology. Official opinion in that country reasoned that since abstract structural relations, not concrete class relations, lay at the heart of its system, it must be reactionary in its content. More recently, supporters of intellectual trends long popular in Western Europe, such as Marxism and phenomenology, have campaigned vigorously—and, for the most part, successfully—against the structuralist view of language. Even in France, at the very moment when structuralism as an intellectual movement was at its peak, structural *linguistics* was hardly any more influential than it had been thirty years earlier. It was, and continues to be, an insignificant force outside of the Sorbonne, where André Martinet has developed an important structuralist program, and a few other institutions. Adam Schaff, the Polish Marxist known for his work in semantics, has remarked on "the number of variations of structuralism which proliferate in France, with genuine structural linguistics having the smallest repercussions in the literature of the subject, and being probably the least known of all."[7]

Indeed, it was only in the United States and Britain that structural linguistics actually gained in influence during and after the Second World War. While even as late as the 1950s there were only a handful of independent linguistics departments, their presence and prestige was nevertheless strong enough to allow those with an autonomous orientation to language to capitalize on the university expansion of the next decade. Most departments formed then were controlled from the beginning by autonomous linguists.

Three factors were responsible for the structuralists' success in the United States.[8] First, they found a highly visible issue that served to distinguish them from most other linguistic scholars and around which they could rally. Second, in a time and place in which the prestige of science was at its apex, they were able to project themselves as having the only "scientific" orientation to language. And third, they were able to win the patronage of powerful and wealthy interests who helped to sustain them, both financially and organizationally.

The rallying point for American structural linguists could be called, for want of a better term, "egalitarianism." The essence of this principle for linguistics is that, in some fundamental sense, all of the languages of the world are cut from the same mold. In structuralist terms, this means that all languages and dialects can be analyzed using the same methods, and that there are none whose properties cannot be adequately described in terms of an autonomous structural system. Furthermore, while egalitarianism does not deny that the nature of the system might vary markedly from language to language, it does reject the idea that the complexity of the system correlates in any way with the level of cultural advancement of the speakers. Indeed, structural linguists in general have rejected the idea that grammars can be compared fruitfully in terms of relative complexity.

The most forceful early proponent of egalitarianism in

linguistics was Franz Boas, the first part of whose best-known work, the *Handbook of American Indian Languages*, was published in 1911. Most American anthropologists, as well as linguists, can trace their intellectual lineage to Boas. He campaigned vigorously against claims that the sounds of non-Western languages were vague and variable, thus defying transcription, and that their grammatical structure was incapable of expressing abstract concepts. Boas exposed the transparently ideological nature of these ideas, and painstakingly showed that the grammatical sophistication of non-Western languages is every bit as advanced as that of Western ones.

Propagandizing for the linguistic equality of all languages and dialects became the hallmark of linguistic writing in the United States, both scholarly and popular. Boas's student Edward Sapir expressed the sentiment in his classic book *Language:* "When it comes to linguistic form, Plato walks with the Macedonian swineherd, Confucius with the head-hunting savage of Assam."[9] And to this day, introductory textbooks hammer home the same point. Thus, Fromkin and Rodman's *Introduction to Language* informs the beginning student:

> Although the rules of your grammar may differ from the rules of someone else's grammar, there can't possibly be a mistake in your grammar. This is because according to linguists no language or variety of a language (called a dialect) is superior to any other in a *linguistic* sense. Every grammar is equally complex and logical and capable of producing an infinite set of sentences to express any thought one might wish to express. If something can be ex-

pressed in one language or one dialect, it can be expressed in any other language or dialect. You might use different means and different words, but it can be expressed. Because grammars are what determine the nature of the languages, no grammar is to be preferred except perhaps for nonlinguistic reasons.[10]

From the beginning, American structuralists hit upon egalitarianism as the cause around which they could crystallize their professional identity. According to Leonard Bloomfield, who with Sapir developed American structural linguistics, it was even in part responsible for the decision, in 1924, to found the Linguistic Society of America. Bloomfield hoped that such a society would counteract resistance to the idea that the languages of highly civilized people were on a par with those of "savages," an idea that the average person finds "repugnant to the common sense."[11]

The principle of egalitarianism, so central to American linguistics, did not play a significant role in the development of structural linguistics in Europe.* While the Europeans generally accepted the principle, they never made it an issue around which they could distinguish themselves professionally. As a matter of fact, a number of continental linguists were actively hostile to it. In 1948, the Dutch comparativist J. Gonda wrote that the comparative method was inapplicable to "primitive" languages like those of the Indonesian family, a view immediately blasted by the American structuralist

---

* Though it was a driving force behind other varieties of European structuralism (e.g., Lévi-Strauss's challenge to ethnocentrism in anthropology).

George Trager as "a counsel of despair, where it is not sheer ethnocentric racism,"[12] and as recently as 1964 the Swedish structuralist Bertil Malmberg remarked that structural principles would have to be applied in different ways to literary and nonliterary languages.[13]

As long as American structuralists confined their campaign to the languages of remote tribes, they did little to upset their colleagues in departments of modern and classical languages—in which almost all linguists were situated in the interwar years. But such was certainly not the case when they began crusading for the linguistic equality of *all* dialects of English and other literary languages, no matter how "substandard" they were regarded. This egalitarian view came in direct conflict with the long-seated tradition in the humanities that values a language variety in direct proportion to its literary output. A number of linguists from this period have commented on the difficulties they experienced in literature departments. According to Edgar Sturtevant, the annual summer institutes sponsored by the Linguistic Society of America grew in size because the vast majority of linguists found themselves in departments staffed by people who had "little understanding or sympathy for linguists and whom the linguist had to appease in order to stay employed."[14] Another linguist active since the 1930s notes that "although a handful of language-and-literature departments welcomed linguists, the great majority were uncompromisingly hostile."[15] The atmosphere was such that Zellig Harris, probably the leading American linguist after Sapir and Bloomfield, could not teach linguistics in his own Oriental Languages department at Pennsylvania. Rather he had to do so in Anthropology, "under the guise of analysis of unwritten languages."[16]

The attempt to bring the idea of linguistic equality to the general public met with similar resistance. As a result of their egalitarian refusal to denigrate nonstandard varieties of English, and their consequent opposition to prescriptive grammar, structural linguists have been perceived as sabotaging the language, and cultural standards and values in general. As recently as 1950, the American structuralist Robert Hall was forced to publish privately a book that defended the linguistic value of all dialects, standard and nonstandard alike: no publisher wished to be associated with such a position. Doubleday took it on ten years later only after it had proved its salability and only after Hall had changed its title from the inflammatory-sounding *Leave Your Language Alone!* to the neutral *Linguistics and Your Language.* In 1964, the Linguistic Society of America reported to the National Commission on the Humanities that the recent advances in linguistics had "essentially zero" effect on the general public, and that "a fair proportion of highly educated laymen see in linguistics the great enemy of all they hold dear."[17] The accusations come from all different quarters. Thus, the historian Jacques Barzun, for example, charges modern linguists with a "grave responsibility . . . for the state of the language as we find it in centers of culture."[18] And recent reports documenting the declining academic performance of America's schoolchildren have intensified the hostility even more. Editorial writers point accusing fingers at professional linguists, whose rampant "permissiveness" is seen as a major factor contributing to the decline.

43

Indeed, structural linguists have opened themselves to the charge. Their commitment to egalitarianism has led them to dissociate themselves from prescriptive grammar—the idea that "correct" speech forms should be prescribed. While many of their European counterparts, far from opposing prescriptive grammar, have gone so far as to put themselves at the service of the academies and commissions set up in continental countries to "regulate" the national language, American linguists have consistently rejected the idea that it is their role to act as prescriptive grammarians, and they have gleefully exposed the flimsy and politically charged bases of many such prescriptions.

Prescriptive grammar has a fascinating history. As the linguist Geoffrey Nunberg shows, its eighteenth-century origins lay firmly in classical liberal thought:

> From its inception, then, the modern doctrine of good usage was associated with liberal ideals, in its insistence that linguistic values were best decided in the free discourse of men of learning and good sense, whatever their birth or station. That association continued until the first half of this century, as people like Orwell, Auden, and Lionel Trilling continued to defend traditional linguistic values. It is only lately, as the doctrines of grammar have come to be regarded as a rigid code, that conservatives have become its champions.[19]

Nunberg attributes the transformation of prescriptive grammar into the bulwark of conservatism to the rise of mass education and the collapse of the homogeneous social elite that had dominated mores and culture until the First World War:

> For working-class students, and more recently, for members of ethnic and racial minorities, the mastery of "correct English" entails a good deal more than learning the traditional rules of pronoun agreement and the like. They must learn to master the habits of middle-class speech that the traditional grammarians had always presumed. And those habits, unlike the traditional rules, have no rational justification. . . . Inevitably, schoolteachers found themselves spending more time teaching rules of usage that had no basis in the rational program of traditional grammar, but only in invidious distinctions of class and race.[20]

And class and race are not the only issues. Consider the following from drama critic and pop grammarian John Simon, who boasts about his lack of knowledge of linguistics,[21] and whose advocacy of prescriptive "good grammar" barely masks his right-wing positions. Simon exhorts: "Don't let fanatical feminists convince you that it must be 'as he or she pleases,' which is clumsy and usually serves no other purpose than that of placating the kind of extremist who does not deserve to be placated."[22] The only thing keeping Simon's claim that Black English is the language of "ignorant, misguided, or merely lazy creatures for whom making distinctions is an unnecessary effort"[23] from being a fully articulated racist theory is that he does not explicitly attribute the "ignorance" of blacks to their genetic inheritance.

But if structural linguists have insisted on the equality of nonstandard dialects, they have certainly not been reluctant to urge people to accommodate to prescriptive norms. Robert Hall sees the distinction:

> Often enough, we may find the need to change our usage, simply because social and financial success depends on some norm, and our speech is one of the things that will be used as a norm. In a situation like this, it is advisable to make the adjustment; but let's do so on the basis of actual social acceptability of our speech. . . .[24]

The content of Hall's remarks is that however equal dialects may be in theory, they are not equal in practice. Most American structuralists have been as vociferous as anyone else in appealing to nonstandard speakers to imitate the dominant standard—but on different grounds. Still, one wonders if the mixed message they have broadcast ("nonstandard dialects are fine, but . . .") is not responsible, at least in part, for the public hostility to their basic tenet that such dialects are linguistically on a par with the standard.

Despite the scorn American structuralism suffered for its egalitarian outlook, in the long run this commitment had a positive effect on its growth. By holding on to an issue that would always keep it in the public eye, structural linguistics was able to maintain a visibility that helped both to recruit bright students into its ranks and to compete successfully for its share of support. In the competitive American academic environment, where one's position is often a function of how successfully one's ideas are advertised, the structural linguists were successful in capturing attention.

A second distinguishing characteristic of American structural linguistics in the 1940s and 1950s was its self-definition as the only "scientific" orientation to language. It is impossible to overemphasize the importance of this claim to its success. In this period, to bear the mantle of "science" in the United States guaranteed admiration and prestige, and structural linguistics was regarded as that branch of the humanities that had come closest to achieving results comparable to those of the natural sciences. As one commentator put it, American structural linguistics "could be compared in method with field physics, quantum mechanics, discrete mathematics, and Gestalt psychology."[25]

The conception of what it meant for something to be "scientific" in this period was thoroughly empiricist. Like their colleagues in philosophy and the social sciences, many leading structuralist linguists in this country were committed to incorporating empiricist assumptions into their theory. The American pioneer in this respect was Leonard Bloomfield, who produced an entire monograph devoted to illustrating the intimate relationship of empiricist philosophy, behaviorist psychology, and American structural linguistics.[26] Those American structuralists in the 1940s and 1950s most faithful to Bloomfield's program attempted to reconstitute structural linguistics along strict empiricist lines. Their goal was to devise a set of mechanical procedures whereby the phonemes, morphemes, and syntactic categories in a language could literally be extracted from the raw data without any recourse to nonobservables and without any need for the linguist's own intuition about how to proceed.

By hitching his fortunes to "science," Bloomfield assured that he and his followers would come to dominate structural linguistics in America. Those who resisted the empiricist tide, like Sapir and his students, found themselves increasingly uninfluential in discussions about linguistic theory and methodology.* And by the 1950s, the Bloomfieldians had proved so successful that those taking a strictly humanistic approach to language in the United States had ceased altogether to be regarded as "linguists"—a state of affairs that still holds true today.

Their empiricist outlook contributed to the success of the American structuralists in another, more indirect way. Since it dissuaded them from raising the broad fundamental questions about the nature of language (or the relationship between language and other phenomena), they kept to a single-minded focus on developing procedures for phonemic and morphemic analysis. Hence, a group of "specialists" arose in America whose only professional loyalty was to the field of linguistics and its particular techniques.

Nowhere were the practical consequences of the American empiricist stance more evident than in the treatment of "meaning." To the Europeans, the understanding of the role of language in conveying meaning was paramount; consequently they devoted considerable atten-

---

* The essence of the intellectual differences between Sapir and Bloomfield can be captured nicely by Bloomfield's sobriquet for Sapir—"medicine man"—and by Sapir's references to "Bloomfield's sophomoric psychology."[27]

tion to the semantic function of the units they arrived at in their structural analysis. Their preoccupation with meaning meant that they were constantly abutting on fields like philosophy, psychology, or criticism that also studied meaning. Paradoxically their interdisciplinary interests diminished their commitment to building linguistics as an independent discipline. Some American structural linguists, on the other hand, attempted to expunge the study of meaning altogether from the field of linguistics. They felt uncomfortable even addressing a concept so notoriously difficult to quantify and operationalize. Yet the very limitation of their vision helped them create a distinct field with clearly defined boundaries.

To those American structuralist theoreticians who strongly supported the empiricist orientation, European linguistic scholarship seemed more like mysticism than science. Robert Hall puts it with an intensity of feeling typical of his group:

The present-day intellectual atmosphere of Europe is influenced by an essentially reactionary hostility to objective science, and by a return to doctrines of "spiritual activity," "creativity of the human soul," and socially biased value-judgments which European scholarship has inherited from the aristocratic, theological background of mediaeval and Renaissance intellectualism. This reactionary attitude is present in the theorizing of many modern European students of language, who sacrifice positive analysis of concrete data to discussion of purely imaginary, non-demonstrable fictions like "thought" and "spirit" as supposedly reflected in language. In American work on language, the burning question at present is whether this same anti-scientific attitude is to be allowed to block the further development of linguistics and its contribution to our understanding of human affairs, especially in our teaching.[28]

Leo Spitzer, a European exile then teaching in the United States, in turn accused Hall of desiring to set up an "academic F.B.I." to stifle views departing from those currently fashionable in America.[29]

Certainly a large share of the American animosity toward European linguistics in the period immediately before and during the Second World War was based on genuine differences about the nature of linguistic research. But it cannot be denied that the Americans' feeling was fueled by more personal resentments. Many Americans felt that positions for which they were qualified were being given instead to European refugees. Their anger, of course, was easily understandable in the Depression days, when jobs were scarce. Robert Hall remembers frequently hearing leading American theoreticians boast as if in compensation: "We'll show those Europeans we have something they never dreamed of."[30]

By the end of the 1940s, however, as a result of increased transatlantic scholarly contact after World War II, signs of rapprochement appeared on both sides. In 1951, we find an extremely favorable review by the American Charles Hockett of a book by the leading French structuralist, André Martinet, and Martinet in turn writing that terminological differences alone were the major impediment to Americans and Europeans understanding each other's work.[31]

The third, and probably most important, reason for the success of structural linguistics in the United States is that the American government, early on, found it in its interest, directly or indirectly, to sponsor structuralist research. The special relationship between the government and the profession, which began on the eve of the Second World War, was so vital for the field that it has even been suggested that "'American structuralism' was shaped in the post-war period by field work experience directed, not toward anthropology, but toward the international involvements of the United States."[32]

The relationship began in 1939, as a result of ideas proposed by Mortimer Graves, then executive secretary of the American Council of Learned Societies (ACLS), one of the major American organizations providing grants to academics. Graves was profoundly impressed with the results that the structural linguists had achieved in analyzing unwritten American Indian languages, and reasoned that they would meet with equal success in the analysis of languages that were likely to be of strategic importance in the worldwide conflict he considered inevitable.[33] Furthermore, the structuralists themselves were convinced, and were successful in convincing others, that their methods of analysis were directly applicable to the preparation of the language instruction manuals and grammars that the American forces would need. Indeed, they boasted that one of the greatest virtues of the structuralist approach to language, as opposed to other approaches, was that it lent itself directly to pedagogical applications. The "linguistic method of language teaching," as they called it, consisted in large part of drilling the student directly in the structural patterns that resulted from their analyses.

As a consequence of the widely accepted view that America's structural linguists had "solved" the problem of how to teach languages, it was to them that the government turned in its hour of need, rather than to linguists of other orientations.

In 1941, with $100,000 from the Rockefeller Foundation, the ACLS organized the Intensive Language Program (ILP), and appointed J Milton Cowan, then secretary treasurer of the Linguistic Society of America, as director. By the summer of 1943, the ILP conducted fifty-six courses, in twenty-six languages, at eighteen universities, for some seven hundred students. When the ILP was terminated at the end of the war, it was estimated that every trained linguist in the United States had been involved in it.*

Graves's organizational skill in providing funding, employment, and research opportunities to the linguists of the United States was a major factor in the development of the field, and was regarded as bearing equal responsibility for the success of American structural linguistics as the work of Boas, Sapir, Bloomfield, and Whorf.[35]

Almost immediately after America entered the war, the

---

* In an interesting sidelight, Hymes and Fought suggest that the wartime concentration of the leading figures in American linguistics in one building — 165 Broadway in New York City — working on language teaching materials for the United States army, may well have been the major factor responsible for the distinct empiricist and xenophobic character of American structural linguistics in this period.[34]

Army, through the American Council of Learned Societies, turned to the Linguistic Society for professional services.[36] As early as 1942, the journal *Hispania* observed "that the Director [of the ILP, J Milton Cowan] is constantly called upon for advice on language problems by practically every agency of the Government which has these problems: Office of Strategic Services, Board of Economic Welfare, Department of Justice, as well as the numerous departments of the Army, Navy, and Marine Corps."[37]

The most visible products of the joint government-ACLS-LSA work during the war were "useful" materials: pocket language guides and accompanying records in fifty-six languages, and complete self-teaching language courses in thirty languages. But theoretical linguistics as well reaped the bounty of the all but unlimited governmental subvention. Martin Joos noted in his anthology of American structural linguistics that "in the hothouse atmosphere of the wartime work, American linguistic theory was to develop far more swiftly than it had before."[38] The results of this development jammed the printing presses after wartime restrictions on publishing scholarly material had been lifted. Fully one-third of the papers in Joos's reader, which covered American structuralism through 1956, were published in the three years following the war. Two of the major contributions of American linguistics, Bloomfield's *Outline Guide for the Practical Study of Foreign Languages* and Bloch and Trager's *Outline of Linguistic Analysis*, were originally published by the ILP and then reissued by the United States Armed Forces Institute. And Robert Hall directly attributes the founding of the journals *Studies in Linguistics, Word,* and *Romance*

Philology to the "quickened activity of linguists during the war period."[39]

After the war, the Language Training Program of the Foreign Service Institute (FSI) of the State Department filled the void left by the termination of the ILP and other war-connected programs. The FSI, founded in 1947, had its origin in the realization "that the new role which the United States was destined to play in world affairs required competence of the highest order on the part of those engaged in the conduct of foreign relations."[40] The general objective of its language and area specializations (under which linguistics was taught) was that the Foreign Service officer "should acquire a thorough understanding of foreign peoples and should develop effective ways of communicating with them in aiding the implementation of national policy."[41] Here, while enrolled in such courses as "Public Opinion Formation in Foreign Countries," "Economic Development of Underdeveloped Countries," and "Oil and the Middle East," the future diplomat, career officer, or foreign administrator could also study linguistic theory under some of America's most prominent structural linguists. One should not underestimate the FSI's importance to the field; in an overview of the linguistic profession, the educational psychologist John B. Carroll noted that in order to support their language-teaching program, the School of Languages and Linguistics of the FSI became "one of the major centers of linguistic research in the United States."[42]

The Cold War added a new, blatantly imperialistic motivation for the support of linguistic research. Mortimer Graves, in his plea for more government funding, explained why studies of the "multifarious cultures" outside our borders were vital to our national interest:

> The product of American industry spreads all over the world. Wherever there is a paved road there is an American automobile; American oil is produced wherever there is oil and used wherever oil is used. American banks have branches and connections in every significant foreign city. Hardly a remote corner of the globe but knows the American missionary, the American school, American generosity. . . . Half the world's trains run on American rails. No region is too remote to be the concern of American diplomacy. And all too frequently American armed forces must ply their trade in lands and among peoples whose very names would have been unknown to an earlier generation.
>
> One would suppose accordingly that many Americans would be equipped with scientific and detailed understanding of these multifarious cultures, that the United States would lead the world in the study of foreign lands no matter how distant, that no society could be named for which there was not an American expert, and that the American academic structure would reflect this world perspective. Unfortunately, a true picture is almost the reverse of this. . . . Study of many culturally and strategically important peoples finds no place whatever in American universities and colleges.[43]

Linguistics, according to Graves, is more than just one component of this study; it is a major weapon in the Cold War:

Ideological World War III has started and there is no certainty that it is well won yet. In spite of the fact that this is a war for men's minds, there exist no Joint Chiefs of Staff planning such a war, no war production authority concerning itself with material for such a war. These questions are by and large, in our society, left to the private initiative of the type that one sees in the Georgetown Institute of Languages and Linguistics.

In this war for men's minds, obviously the big guns of our armament is [sic] competence in languages and linguistics.[44]

The passage of the National Defense Education Act in 1958 was a shot in the arm for the field of linguistics. Title IV gave a great number of linguistics graduate students financial support, while Title VI provided for language teachers' institutes, language and area centers, fellowships for language study, and language research. Actually, all four of the Title VI programs included basic linguistic research, the most sizable being a $650,000 grant for the study of the Ural-Altaic languages spoken in the Soviet Union. There is no doubt that this level of support for linguistic research was intended to continue only as long as linguists could convince the federal government that their findings would aid language teaching, particularly of the "critical languages." Albert Marckwardt emphasized this fact and commented that if structural linguists "fail to live up to the claims they have made for their science [about its applicability to language teaching] — often too vociferously and without due modesty and caution — they may have muffed the chance for once and all. It is no exaggeration to say that the NDEA has put linguistics squarely on the spot. 'Put up or shut up' may be a crude phrase, but it describes the situation precisely."[45] Kenneth W. Mildenberger, chief of the Language Development Section of the United States Office of Education, explained that while his office had no formal policy directed toward linguistics, it did have an "*attitude*" about the intent and spirit of all the programs covered by the National Defense Education Act. Their "mission" was to strengthen and extend language instruction "to meet the needs of the national interest."[46] He then repeated Marckwardt's threat to linguists to "put up or shut up."

This special governmental support of linguistic research, so significant to the development of the field in the United States, had an equivalent only in Great Britain. Indeed, in Britain, the links between the government and the linguistic profession were forged long before the Second World War. As early as 1798, the Marquess of Wellesley, then the governor-general of India, had proposed an institute to study the languages and cultures of the Empire. This project came to fruition in 1917, with the founding of the School of Oriental Studies—now the School of Oriental and African Studies (SOAS)—in London. The idea was to create an institution "adequate to the needs of an Empire which contains nearly four hundred million Orientals." At the opening ceremony, Sir John Hewitt, chairman of the school's governing body, explained to His Majesty King George V why such an institution was necessary:

> *First*, to provide a place where our young men who will presently be engaged in governing or garrisoning the Oriental and African parts of the Empire

may learn the languages and study the literature, the religions, and the customs of the peoples with whom they will so soon be brought into contact, and their influence over whom will largely depend upon their familiarity with indigenous character, ideas, and institutions.

Secondly, to offer a training to those who are about to proceed to the same countries to take part in commercial enterprise or other avocations, or for purposes of study and research.

Thirdly, to furnish to the Capital of the Empire a meeting-ground and focus for scholars from the East of various nationalities, where, on their visits to this country, they may be assured of a sympathetic welcome, and find at hand, if they desire them, opportunities for study among those engaged in kindred pursuits.[47]

SOAS became the major center for linguistic research in Great Britain. Because its goals included the study of the cultures as well as the languages of the people over whom the British had "influence," a great deal of linguistic research with humanistic and sociological orientations has taken place at SOAS. However, structural linguistics also received a healthy share of the funds, and as in America, it came into its own during World War II. The British government's demands for more experts in the languages of the people with whom British military personnel would come in contact led to an expanded role for SOAS in general, and significantly shifted the balance toward pure grammatical research. Many of those who mastered techniques of structural analysis under wartime conditions at SOAS went on to form the first faculties of linguistics and phonetics at North Wales, Glasgow, Leeds, Manchester, and elsewhere.[48]

After the government, the most important force supporting structuralism in the United States and, to a lesser extent, in Britain has been the church. Christian missionaries had been active as early as the sixteenth century in preparing word lists and grammatical descriptions of the languages of the conquered peoples in European colonial empires. But in the past forty years, their influence has increased to such a degree that, surprising as it may seem, they now play a major role in linguistic studies. Their involvement stems directly from the goal of evangelical Christianity: to convert all the people of the world to Christian beliefs. The cornerstone of such beliefs is the word as revealed in the Holy Bible. The Bible, however, has not been translated into half of the world's languages; indeed, most of these languages as yet are not written at all. Since a good analysis of a language greatly facilitates the creation of a writing system for it and subsequent translation into it, such analyses have become important preliminary steps to the process of Christianizing.

Several organizations practice linguistic research as a preliminary to Bible translation, but none can compare in size, influence, and visibility to the Summer Institute of Linguistics (SIL). As of 1978, SIL had 3,700 members working on 675 languages in twenty-nine countries, and it is still growing. Since its beginnings in the late 1930s, SIL has published thousands of books, journal articles, and technical reports on linguistic matters. Some of the major figures in American structural linguistics have been affiliated with it; indeed, it is a rare year that the executive committee of the Linguistic Society of America does not contain at least one SIL member. Moreover, SIL today sends more members abroad than any other Protestant missionary society.

"The personnel that makes up SIL," writes Eunice V. Pike, one of the organization's most prominent members, "has the one uniting factor—the belief that every person should be able to have the New Testament in his own language. In addition to that belief each member feels that he is in part responsible to bring that goal to completion."[49] The result is that in many parts of the world the field of linguistics is literally identified with SIL. As one commentator put it, the "army [of SIL members] covers more territory than that occupied by the combined forces of all other linguists."[50]

The SIL enterprise has been accompanied by intense political controversy. To carry out its work, SIL must get the sanction of the government where the targeted language is located. Since a Third World government, whether Catholic and conservative or anticlerical and radical, will naturally have misgivings about an overtly evangelical North American Protestant group working in its midst, SIL presents itself abroad as a purely scientific and cultural organization. (Its missionary aims are revealed, however, in the name it uses to raise funds from the faithful back home: Wycliffe Bible Translators.) Moreover, although SIL has a policy of never opposing the government of any country where it operates, it has on several occasions found itself expelled after a change of regime.

The political orientation of SIL is staunchly conservative (the identification of Communism with Satan is a consistent theme in its writings), and charges abound that it has, on numerous occasions, acted on behalf of one or another national government, particularly when that government's immediate interests have coincided with American foreign policy designs. Indeed, there are charges that SIL has gone so far as to put its resources at the disposal of U.S.-based multinational corporations and the CIA. In addition, many feel that SIL's practice has been to "Americanize" as much as to Christianize, thereby hastening the destruction of the indigenous culture in areas in which it operates.

SIL, for its part, denies the accusations of political involvement. It furthermore insists that its effect on the culture of indigenous groups has been positive. SIL points with pride to its role in literacy campaigns in the Third World and claims to help soften the shock that indigenous people suffer when confronted with Western civilization by providing them with the skills that they will need in order to cope in an alien society.

While the controversy surrounding the organization is unlikely to diminish in the coming years, it is undoubtedly true that SIL's "army," through which 20,000 recruits have passed since 1938, has given American structural linguistics an international presence that structuralism elsewhere could never hope to achieve.[51]

In summary, several important factors—the focus on egalitarianism, the prestige of science, the support of the government and the church, —combined to give structural linguistics a preeminent position in the United States by the mid-1950s, a position that it had failed to achieve on the European continent. In this American context, a new theory of linguistic structure was to appear; a theory wholly within the autonomous linguistic tradition, yet at the same time breaking with many of the fundamental assumptions of the earlier structuralist approaches. It is to that theory, Noam Chomsky's "transformational generative grammar," that we now turn.

4

THE CHOMSKYAN REVOLUTION

" THE extraordinary and traumatic impact of the publication of *Syntactic Structures* by Noam Chomsky in 1957 can hardly be appreciated by one who did not live through this upheaval." So writes the psychologist Howard Maclay in an overview of American linguistics since the 1930s. According to John Lyons, Britain's most prominent linguist, Chomsky's first book, "short and relatively nontechnical though it was, revolutionized the scientific study of language." And the historian of linguistics R. H. Robins concurs that "the description and analysis of language was thrown into exciting turmoil by the publication of Noam Chomsky's *Syntactic Structures*."[1]

What was there in *Syntactic Structures* that would trigger "turmoil" and "trauma" in the normally staid world of academic scholarship? Quite simply, Chomsky overturned all the previous approaches to language, from the ancient Greeks' to those of his own structuralist teachers, and challenged the reigning assumptions about linguistic research, both empiricist and nonempiricist alike.

Chomsky's conceptual break with the American structuralists was not over the question of whether linguistics should be a "science"—he never questioned that it should be—but over the more fundamental issue of what a scientific theory is and how one might be constructed with respect to linguistic phenomena. Chomsky's earliest books and papers are filled with polemics against the empiricist conception of science held by the structural linguists of this country, which led them to attempt to devise a set of procedures designed to extract a grammar from raw linguistic data. Chomsky argued at length that no scientific theory had ever resulted from the scientist performing mechanical operations on the data. How the scientist happens to hit upon a particular theoretical notion is simply irrelevant; all that counts is its adequacy in explaining the phenomena in its domain.

Chomsky's rejection of empiricist constraints on theory formation led him to propose a novel conception of what a linguistic theory is a theory *of*. Whereas to earlier structuralists, a theory of language was no more than a concise taxonomy of the elements extractable from a corpus of data, Chomsky redefined the goal of linguistic theory to that of providing a rigorous and formal characterization of a "possible human language," that is, to distinguishing as precisely as possible the class of grammatical processes that can occur in language from those that cannot. This characterization, which Chomsky later came to call "universal grammar," specifies the limits within which all languages function. In Chomsky's view, natural scientists set parallel tasks for themselves: the goal of physicists is to characterize the class of possible physical processes, that of biologists to characterize the class of possible biological processes, and so on.

While most structuralists had tended to ignore syntax, in the Chomskyan view of language, syntactic relations are central. Indeed, the grammar of a language is represented by a formal set of rules that "generate" (i.e., specify explicitly) the possible sentences and their associated structural properties. Hence the term "generative grammar" is applied to the theory as a whole and its advocates are called "generativists." In most formulations of the theory, syntactic processes in language can be described by two types of rules: phrase structure rules and transformational rules. The former type divide a sentence into its component phrases; an English example of a phrase structure rule is S → NP AUX VP, which is read: "A sentence consists of a noun phrase followed by an auxiliary followed by a verb phrase." The effect of this rule can be illustrated by the sentence *the train might be late; the train* is a noun phrase, *might* is an auxiliary, and *be late* is a verb phrase. Transformational rules relate sentence types. For example, the transformational rule of Passive makes explicit the structural parallels between sentence types such as *John threw the ball* and *the ball was thrown by John,* the rule of *Wh*-Movement does the same for such sentence types as *John saw who?* and *who did John see?* and so on. Transformational rules have played such an important role that the theory is often referred to as "transformational generative grammar" or even simply as "transformational grammar."

The grammatical analysis of a sentence (its "derivation") involves, first, the application of the phrase structure rules. These rules produce the *deep structure* of the sentence—the level at which the basic syntactic relations between its elements are represented in their simplest form. The transformational rules then change that deep structure into the sentence's *surface structure*—the sentence as it is actually spoken. For many years, generativists assumed that the deep structure of a sentence is the syntactic level most directly correlated with its meaning.[2] However, in recent years, Chomsky and most others have come to believe that surface structure as well plays an important function in semantic interpretation.

In the late 1950s, Chomsky, in collaboration with Morris Halle, began to develop a theory of generative phonology as well.[3] The phonological rules account for the sound patterning of the language, from simple phenomena, such as the alternation between unaspirated and aspirated "p" described in the preceding chapter, to far more complex ones, such as the alternation between the "k" and "s" sounds in pairs like *electric-electricity* and *opaque-opacity.*

The following diagram then, represents schematically Chomsky's conception of the organization of the grammatical model:

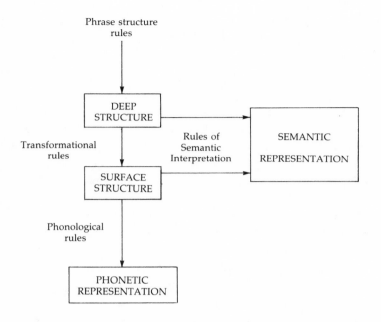

It is a principle of universal grammar that languages do not differ in the way their grammars are organized — i.e., the grammars of all languages are constructed in accordance with the diagram above. Proposals about the nature of universal grammar have been refined in great detail. Generativists now believe that universal grammar specifies not just the overall shape of the grammar but even the form the rules may take. For example, it has been observed that in no language is it natural in everyday speech to question a proper subpart of a coordinate construction (i.e., a construction in which two words or phrases are linked by a conjunction — *John and Mary, the big dog and the little cat*, and *the table or the chair* are examples of such constructions). In other words, a sentence like *What did John eat beans and?*, understood as a question whose appropriate response could be *John ate beans and rice*, is impossible, outside of unusual contexts such as children's games. This has led to a proposed addition to universal grammar called the "Coordinate Structure Constraint,"[4] which prohibits the grammar of any language from containing a transformational rule whose operation involves questioning a word in a coordinate construction.

The Chomskyan approach to grammar helped solve numerous problems that had defied treatment earlier. Two are worth mentioning briefly—one from syntax, one from phonology. It had always been problematic how to characterize the ordering of the elements that can occur in the English auxiliary. Notice, for example, that in the sentence *John has been working*, perfect aspect is represented by the combination of the verbal element *has* and the suffix *-en*, which is attached to the following *be-*, while progressive aspect is represented by the combination of *be-* and the *-ing* suffix which is attached to the verb *work*. Furthermore, the *has* and its accompanying *-en* and the *be* and its accompanying *-ing must* cooccur; one cannot say *John has be working* or *John has been work*. In other words, the perfect and progressive morphemes are both discontinuous and overlapping:

John has be en work ing

PERFECT PROGRESSIVE

Structuralist grammars could not deal with this sort of complexity. Since their grammars were simply taxonomic inventories of elements, they had no way of associating the *has* with the noncontiguous *-en* or the *be* with the noncontiguous *-ing;* Chomsky, however, showed that if the grammar consisted of abstract generative rules, the entire distribution of English auxiliary elements could be captured. One simple phrase structure rule, in his analysis, generates as units the two parts of the perfect and progressive morphemes, and a simple transformational rule places them in the discontinuous positions in which they occur in actual speech.

A problem of long standing in phonology was English word stress. Sometimes the heaviest stress falls on the last syllable (*impéde*), sometimes on the next to last (*reprísal*), sometimes on the third from last (*ingrátitude*), and sometimes on the first (*álimony*). We even find different syllables stressed in words with identical roots: *télegraph, telegráphic, telégraphy.* This seemingly chaotic state of affairs forced structuralists to conclude that, unlike word stress in French, German, or Spanish, English word stress is unpredictable. But Chomsky (in collaboration with Morris Halle and Fred Lukoff) demonstrated that given the possibility of interacting abstract phonological rules, English word stress turns out to be largely predictable.

It should be clear then that Chomsky did not challenge the idea that the grammar of a language can be characterized as an autonomous structural system. Far from it. By proposing a structural treatment of relations that hold between sentences (such as between *John threw the ball* and *the ball was thrown by John*), where most had believed that such a treatment was not possible, his approach expanded the scope of autonomous linguistics. Chomsky's work is therefore firmly within the "structuralist" tradition in linguistics. Confusingly, in the early 1960s

Chomsky and his followers began to apply the label "structuralist" just for the earlier autonomous approaches, reserving the term "generativists" for themselves. The result is that now within linguistics, when one speaks of a "structuralist," it is understood that one is referring to an anti-Chomskyan. However, commentators outside the field have always labeled Chomsky a structuralist, and we find his ideas discussed in most overviews of twentieth-century structuralism.[5] This terminological muddle is unfortunate, but, by now, beyond remedy.

As a structuralist (in the broad sense), Chomsky has always been insistent on the validity of the distinction between *langue* and *parole,* which by 1965 he had come to call "competence" and "performance" respectively. Chomsky chose to coin new terms rather than retain Saussure's since he wished to underscore two important differences between competence and *langue:* competence encompasses all syntactic relations in language, while *langue* does not, and competence is characterized by a set of generative rules, rather than by an inventory of elements.

The domain of competence for Chomsky is the autonomous grammar itself and nothing more. The linguistic phenomena studied by sociological and humanistic linguists, in Chomsky's view, fall primarily within the domain of performance. While Chomsky has had little to say about the social and aesthetic aspects of language, he has always insisted that they involve a complex interaction between principles of the autonomous grammar and external factors. Hence, Chomsky's approach to language as a whole must be understood as "interactionist" rather than "reductionist."

One might wonder at this point why Chomsky so rapidly became known outside of linguistics, even before his political views gained him a wide audience. After all, the correct form of the theory of grammar is a topic of little interest for the nonspecialist. The reason is that from the beginning, Chomsky and his coworkers called attention to the theory's psychological and philosophical implications. Chomsky first described generative grammar as a cognitive model in his 1959 review of B. F. Skinner's *Verbal Behavior*.[6] Pointing to the complexity of language and the amazing speed with which it is acquired, Chomsky concluded that children could not possibly be born "blank slates," as Skinner and other behaviorists would have it; rather they must have a genetic predisposition to structure the acquisition of linguistic knowledge in a highly specific way. In short, the grammar constructed by the linguist is literally "in the head" of the speaker.

Chomsky's review has come to be regarded as one of the foundational documents of the discipline of cognitive psychology, and even after the passage of twenty-five years it is considered the most important refutation of behaviorism. Of all his writings, it was the Skinner review that contributed most to spreading his reputation beyond the small circle of professional linguists.

Chomsky also explored the related philosophical implications of generative grammar in his earliest work. As we have already noted, *Syntactic Structures* challenged the empiricist foundations of American structural linguistics. By the publication of *Aspects of the Theory of Syntax* in 1965, Chomsky had come to characterize generative grammar explicitly as a rationalist theory, in the sense that it posits innate principles that determine the form of acquired knowledge. As part of the theory's conceptual apparatus, Chomsky reintroduced two terms long out of fashion in academic discussion: *innate ideas* and *mind*. For Chomsky, "innate ideas" are simply those properties of the grammar that are inborn and constrain the acquisition of language. So, for example, generativists believe that the Coordinate Structure Constraint discussed above is "prewired," so to speak, into the child, rather than acquired through anything we might reasonably call "learning." Hence, the Coordinate Structure Constraint, like other universals of grammar, is an "innate idea."

Generativists typically support innateness claims by pointing to the "poverty of the stimulus" available to the child language learner. How could a child have learned such-and-such a principle inductively, they argue, given its abstractness, the limited amount of relevant information presented to the child, and the speed of acquisition? Thus the innateness-universality of the Coordinate Structure Constraint is supported by the fact that children are not exposed to nearly enough raw speech data to allow them to figure out this highly complex and abstract property of grammars on their own.

A seemingly paradoxical conclusion follows from this argument, namely that a great deal can be learned about universal grammar from the study of just one language. If we make the reasonable assumption that children born into, say, an English speech community are no different from children born into others, then it follows that a detailed analysis of the grammar they acquire will reveal a great deal about the principles guiding language acquisition in general. For example, if the Coordinate Structure Constraint is innate for English-acquiring children, then it follows that it must constrain the grammars of all languages.

"Mind," for Chomsky, refers to the principles, both innate and acquired, that underlie actual behavior. Such principles, obviously, are not restricted to the realm of language. For example, as recent research has shown, many important aspects of the visual system are also "prewired" and need only a triggering experience from the environment to be set in motion. In Chomsky's terms, then, the theory of vision is a rationalist theory, and the structures underlying visual perception (innate ideas) form part of mind.

While mind may encompass more cognitive faculties than language, Chomsky believes that linguistic studies are the best suited of all to reveal the essence of mind. For one thing, language is the one cognitive faculty that is *uniquely* human. Not even the study of the communicative behavior of the lower animals sheds any light on it: the mental structures underlying animal communication seem to bear no evolutionary relation to those underlying human language. Also, language is the vehicle of rational thought—another uniquely human ability. And finally, we know far more about language and how it functions than we do about other aspects of cognition. After all, more than two millennia of grammatical research have given us a more detailed picture of the structure of language than a bare century of research has clarified the nature of vision, memory, concept formation, and so on.

Chomsky is happy to refer to the faculty for language as an aspect of "human nature." The term "human nature" for him has real content: it is characterized by the set of innately endowed capacities for language, other aspects of cognition, and whatever else, which, being innate, are immune to environmental influences. Chomsky sees such a conception in an entirely positive political light: our genetic inheritance — our human nature — prevents us from being plastic, infinitely malleable beings completely subjugable to the whims of outside forces.

In the leftist milieu, claims about innate ideas or, by extension, an innate human nature are invariably regarded as disreputable, and often for good reason. What better rationalization could one find for invidious racial practice or sexual discrimination than the idea that blacks or women are, by their genetic makeup, "innately" preprogrammed to play subservient roles? It is not uncommon for a radical critique of Chomsky's ideas to start — and stop — with the statement that since his conceptions include innate principles and the idea of a substantive human nature, they must therefore be intrinsically unprogressive, or worse. Indeed, judging by the intense critical response evoked by his terms "innate ideas" or "mind," one might think he had summoned up the specter of feudal lords, mitered bishops, and the whole arsenal of reaction. But such conclusions miss a fundamental point. For Chomsky, the innate language capacity is the property of all humans, not just those of one race, sex, class, national group, or whatever. Universal grammar is as much a human property as the possession of two arms, two legs, and a heart. For Chomsky, universal grammar unites all people, it does not divide them. Moreover, Chomsky points out, empiricism—the idea that there exists no innate human nature—is no more intrinsically antithetical to racism than rationalism is conducive to it. Since empiricists do not distinguish, in principle, between accidental and essential human properties—indeed, they reject the idea of the latter—the logic of their position leads them to treat individuals as inferior beings simply because circumstances have placed them in an inferior role. Consistent rationalists, on the other hand, are forced to weigh the contribution of both the circumstantial and the essential for any given case.[7]

The implication that the advocacy of innate human nature entails a reactionary political stance has a special poignancy in the case of Chomsky, who offers an unparalleled example of a consistent commitment to progressive causes. Chomsky was probably the best-known academic critic of the war in Vietnam. His opposition to this "obscenity, a depraved act by weak and miserable men,"[8] which included leadership in Resist, a national draft resistance movement, brought him more public attention than his scholarly contributions ever did. From the start, he attacked not just the war itself but also the liberal technocracy in America, which used progressive-sounding rhetoric to mask its commitment to the foreign policy assumptions that underlay the war. His repeated insistence on the responsibility of the intellectual to expose official hypocrisy has led him to cover topics ranging from the Spanish Civil War to the Middle East and East Timor to the general issue of human rights.[9]

Chomsky identifies himself politically as an anarchosyndicalist; that is, he shares Marx's analysis of capitalism but disagrees with him on the question of state power.[10] As an anarchosyndicalist, he rejects the conception of the intermediate stage of the "dictatorship of the proletariat" as a prerequisite to a communist society. In particular, he wholeheartedly rejects the Leninist conception of the vanguard party, and argues that it leads inevitably to a new ruling class purporting to govern in the name of the workers but in reality oppressing them. Instead, he believes in the necessity for "spontaneous revolutionary action" to establish the nucleus of the alternative institutions that will ultimately replace the capitalist state.

It is fair to ask what these political concerns with spontaneous action have to do with deep structures, grammatical rules, innate constraints governing the acquisition of syntax, and all the other accouterments of generative grammar. Is there any connection at all between Chomsky's linguistic and political views? To be sure, Chomsky himself sees only a tenuous one:

> If there is a connection, it is on a rather abstract level. I don't have access to any unusual methods of analysis, and what special knowledge I have concerning language has no immediate bearing on social and political issues. Everything I have written on these topics could have been written by someone else. There is no very direct connection between my political activities, writing and others, and the work bearing on language structure, though in some measure they perhaps derive from certain common assumptions and attitudes with regard to basic aspects

of human nature. Critical analysis in the ideological arena seems to me to be a fairly straightforward matter as compared to an approach that requires a degree of conceptual abstraction. For the analysis of ideology, which occupies me very much, a bit of open-mindedness, normal intelligence, and healthy skepticism will generally suffice.[11]

What are these "common assumptions and attitudes with regard to basic aspects of human nature"? We may find them in Chomsky's belief that creative self-expression and free control of all aspects of one's life and thought are fundamentally human capacities. Clearly, this characterizes the essence of anarchosyndicalism. But creativity and the possibility of free self-expression are also important themes in his writings on the psychology of language. The principal conclusion of his Skinner review, after all, was that language was independent, free of stimulus control: we do have the ability to use our language in a truly creative way. And the "grammatical rules" so central to Chomsky's theory of language are almost preconditions for the creative use of language:

> I think that true creativity means free action within the framework of a system of rules. In art, for instance, if a person just throws cans of paint randomly at a wall, with no rules at all, no structure, that is not artistic creativity, whatever else it may be. It is a commonplace of aesthetic theory that creativity involves action that takes place within a framework of rules, but is not narrowly determined either by the rules or by external stimuli. It is only when

you have the combination of freedom and constraint that the question of creativity arises.[12]

One can only speculate whether Chomsky's political activism would have drawn the degree of publicity that it has if he had not already become known as the foremost practitioner of an academic specialty. Indeed, in spite of the controversy surrounding it from the beginning, generative grammar quickly rose to prominence in American linguistics: as early as the mid-1960s it was being described as the established "paradigm."[13] How did it attain this position in less than a decade? A number of factors were responsible. First and foremost, a significant number of linguists, particularly young ones, found the premises of Chomsky's theory convincing and its results impressive. After all, Chomsky had succeeded in solving problems of grammatical analysis that empiricist structuralist approaches had wrestled with unsuccessfully for years. The acceptance of Chomsky's ideas was facilitated by the fact that the climate of opinion in the late 1950s was much more conducive to abstract theorizing than it had been a decade before. In that earlier period, empiricism was at its peak, not just in the social sciences but in philosophy as well. But by the 1950s, empiricism had begun to lose its hold in all fields. Even earlier, it had become clear to philosophers that scientific theories were not mere inductive generalizations from the data, as empiricists believed; rather, the relationship between data and theory was typically rather indirect.[14] And as the 1950s progressed, fundamental inadequacies were revealed in the empiricist theories that held sway in both American psychology and sociology.[15] Hence, it is not surprising that in 1957 Chomsky was able to attract an audience for his challenge to the dominant empiricist linguistic theory: the young linguists' attraction to his ideas was enhanced by their excitement at being in the forefront of intellectual life.

It must be admitted, however, that the confrontational style that many early generativists adopted in their writings and in their behavior at public conferences was also very effective at winning over the young. Chomsky himself has always been rather restrained, at least in public. But two of his earliest collaborators, Robert B. Lees and Paul Postal, became legendary for their uncompromising attacks on the work of the "Old Guard." No paper or presentation that betrayed an empiricist orientation to linguistics could get by unscathed. Some of these attacks were nothing less than vicious, going well beyond the norms of scholarly criticism, and were felt to impugn their opponents' intelligence and character as well as their ideas about linguistic research. The mood on the campuses of the 1960s was conducive to the success of a confrontational style. Students who perhaps an hour earlier had raised their voices in anger at a civil rights or antiwar rally, felt an instant identity with a Lees or Postal whose barrage of rhetoric was directed against a generally accepted set of intellectual propositions. The similarities of style between political and linguistic revolutionaries apparently led some students to think that generative grammar must have an intrinsically progressive political content. George Lakoff reports reading "in one report of the French student uprising in 1968 that linguistics became an issue: [pre-Chomskyan] structuralism was identified with institutional rigidity and [Chomsky's] transformationalism with change."[16] As Lakoff notes, "No one who knows anything about the actual content of structuralist and transformationalist theories could believe any such thing." But the enthusiasm was true enough, as was the sense that generativist linguistics was in the vanguard of change.

Certainly many linguists—especially the older ones—were "repelled by the arrogance with which [the generativists'] ideas were propounded."[17] But, on the whole, the established leaders of American structural linguistics did not obstruct Chomsky's progress. While his first two generativist manuscripts were rejected by publishers, all of the subsequent ones were accepted. Almost from the start, Chomsky was touted by the leaders of the field as the brightest and most original of the younger generation of linguists. Speaking invitations for major conferences and departmental colloquia were extended to him in the 1950s, and as early as 1962 he was granted the honor of being one of the five plenary session speakers at that year's International Congress of Linguists.

Chomsky's undeniable ease at getting a hearing has been raised as proof that the "Chomskyan revolution" in linguistics was only an illusion—after all, the argument goes, why would the dominant figures undermine their own position?[18] But such an argument betrays a mistaken view of the history of science; in fact, the Old Guard in a field does *not* generally attempt to suppress revolutionary new ideas, however much they might disagree with them. Rather, they simply do not adopt them. Certainly that was how the establishment dealt with the theories of Newton, Priestley, and Kelvin, among others.

And that perfectly describes the development of the Chomskyan revolution as well. With the exception of Sol Saporta and Robert Stockwell (both of whom were quite young at the time) and only a very few others, the leading structural linguists of the late 1950s did not become generativists. Nevertheless, since 1957, practically the entire body of linguistic literature devoted to general theory has had to take a position (pro or con) on Chomsky's conception of language, and there are very few research papers devoted to grammatical analysis that do not betray his influence. As the philosopher John Searle put it: "Chomsky did not convince the established leaders of the field, but he did something more important, he convinced their graduate students."[19]

And these graduate students were in a unique position to extend Chomsky's influence. In the unprecedented expansion of the American university system during the economic boom of the middle and late 1960s, it hardly mattered that, when this first class of generativist students received their Ph.D.'s in 1965, most of the Old Guard–dominated departments showed little inclination to hire them. Jobs were for the taking in the new departments then being organized at state universities in Illinois, California, Texas, Ohio, Massachusetts, Washington, and elsewhere. Thus practically every early generativist Ph.D. recipient obtained a position at a major university. The theory was not held back in the slightest by the fact that the traditional Ivy League centers of linguistic research—Harvard, Cornell, Yale, Pennsylvania, Brown, and Columbia—were to wait years before hiring their first generative grammarian.

To underscore the role that a booming economy played in the success of Chomsky's theory, one need only think about what the situation would be like if generative grammar had been conceived a quarter century later. Today, when even some of the best students from the best departments find themselves unemployed or marginally employed, these same ideas would take many more years to have an equivalent impact on the field. One has to wonder about the role today's economy plays in slowing the acceptance of revolutionary conceptions in all fields.

The rapid success of the theory was also facilitated by the fact that it was able to draw on the vast resources of the Massachusetts Institute of Technology, where Chomsky was hired in 1956, the year after he received his Ph.D. From the start, linguistics at MIT was affiliated with the Research Laboratory of Electronics, which played an important supportive role in the early years of the program. Originally part of the MIT Radiation Laboratory, where, incidentally, radar was developed during World War II, the RLE continued the work of the Radiation Laboratory after the war under a joint services contract (i.e., a contract under which each of the armed services contributed funds). While the specific makeup of the RLE changed over the years, throughout most of the 1960s it comprised three disciplines: General Physics, Plasma Dynamics, and Communication Sciences and Engineering (which included MIT's acoustics laboratory). When Morris Halle, who had a position with the acoustics laboratory, organized the linguistics Ph.D. program in 1960, it seemed natural to classify linguistics, too, as a "communication science." Linguistics thus came under the purview of the RLE, eligible for funds from the Department of Defense, which paid the overhead, student support, and even a portion of faculty salaries.

Defense Department funding was quite helpful to early generative grammar. Most grants went to "think tanks" like the RAND Corporation, the MITRE Corporation, and System Development Corporation, which sought to use formal grammar to help develop such things as computer-aided translation of languages and question-answering systems.* Two large defense grants, however, went directly to generativist research in university linguistics departments: one to MIT in the mid-1960s and the other, a few years later, to UCLA. In a 1971 interview, Colonel Edmund P. Gaines, director of systems design and development at the Air Force's Hanscom Field, gave these reasons for funding linguistic research projects:

> The Air Force has an increasingly large investment in so called "command and control" computer systems. Such systems contain information about the status of our forces and are used in planning and executing military operations. For example, defense of the continental United States against air and missile attack is possible in part because of the use of such computer systems. And of course, such systems support our forces in Vietnam.
>
> The data in such systems is processed in response

---

* It is no more than a myth, albeit a persistent one,[20] that Chomsky tailored his ideas about grammatical analysis to meet the needs of machine translation. Chomsky was indeed a member of a machine translation research team in the mid 1950s, but he left it in short order due to his lack of interest in its ongoing work.

to questions and requests by commanders. Since the computer cannot "understand" English, the commanders' queries must be translated into a language that the computer can deal with; such languages resemble English very little, either in their form or in the ease with which they are learned and used. Command and control systems would be easier to use, and it would be easier to train people to use them, if this translation were not necessary. We sponsored linguistic research in order to learn how to build command and control systems that could understand English queries directly. Of course, studies like the UCLA study are but the first step toward achieving this goal. It does seem clear, however, that the successful operation of such systems will depend on insights gained from linguistic research. . . .[21]

Colonel Gaines went on to express the Air Force's "satisfaction" with UCLA's work.

Defense Department funding was a windfall for generative research, but it was not without its price. Critiques of Chomsky's theory from the left have delighted in calling attention to the military support for the early work conducted in it. Several commentators have cited acknowledgments like the following one, at the beginning of Chomsky's *Aspects of the Theory of Syntax*, to bolster their charge that the theory's foundations are "reactionary" or "idealistic":[22]

The research reported in this document was made possible in part by support extended the Massachusetts Institute of Technology, Research Laboratory of Electronics, by the Joint Services Electronics Programs (U.S. Army, U.S. Navy, and U.S. Air Force) under Contract No. DA36-039-AMC-03200(E); additional support was received from the U.S. Air Force (Electronic Systems Division under Contract AF19(628)-2487), the National Science Foundation (Grant GP-2495), the National Institutes of Health (Grant MH-04737-04), and the National Aeronautics and Space Administration (Grant NsG-496).

As one might expect, Chomsky dismisses the charge that the social content of his theory can be deduced from the origins of the funds that support it. Any research carried out at a university in a capitalist society, he argues in turn, whether the immediate source of the funding is the Department of Defense, the Department of Education, the Xerox Corporation, the Ford Foundation, or even public tax dollars, has the same ultimate origin: the surplus value created by labor. Moreover, anyone condemning him for working at MIT, one of America's largest military contractors, and accepting grants from the Department of Defense, would have to condemn Karl Marx for studying at the British Museum (once "the symbol of the most vicious imperialism in the world"[23]) and accepting gifts of money from Engels—whose family made its fortune in the cotton industry.

In any event, with the close of the 1960s the question became moot. Partly as a result of the escalation of the Vietnam War and with it the passage of the Mansfield Amendment to an appropriations bill, which demanded that military expenditures have direct military relevance, and partly from the fact that the computer-based application attempts were not successful—Colonel Gaines's claims to satisfaction notwithstanding—defense support for linguistics at MIT ceased by 1970. Throughout the 1970s the program had to content itself with rather non-lucrative National Institute of Mental Health training grants for its graduate students.

In the 1970s the influence of generative grammar declined. The hegemony of Chomsky's specific ideas within the field was challenged, and generative grammar as a whole lost the considerable prestige it had enjoyed earlier among scholars outside the field of linguistics.

As early as 1970, Chomsky was in a distinct minority among generative grammarians. Most generativists by then had come to identify their work as "generative semantics." Initially, generative semantics distinguished itself from Chomsky's position on some technical points of analysis that seemed to have few, if any, far-ranging implications. Since most prominent generative semanticists were Chomsky's own former students, it is hardly surprising that the first differences were minor. But by the mid-1970s generative semantics had arrived at positions on most linguistic questions that were radically different from Chomsky's.[24] The main theme in its development was a constant broadening of the scope of syntactic description. Generative semanticists first rejected the distinction between syntactic and semantic generalizations, and claimed that meaning relations (such as the synonymy of *John killed Bill* and *John caused Bill to die*, for example) could be handled by transformational rules. Within a few short years, they had proposed that grammatical theory should deal with a wide variety of generalizations about language use as well. For example,

Robin Lakoff tried to incorporate facts about the status of women in English-speaking society into the grammar itself, so that it might account for the strangeness of the sentence *John is Mary's widower* beside the perfectly acceptable *Mary is John's widow.*[25] In short, generative semanticists felt that grammatical theory should be expanded to treat language in its social setting. In their conception, grammar not only generated the sentences of the language with their associated structures, as Chomsky thought; it also specified the social settings under which it might be appropriate to use those sentences.

It is easy to explain the appeal of generative semantics. Generative grammar had focused strictly on syntactic, phonological, and a narrow range of semantic processes; it made no claims at all about the role of language in society, nor its functioning as the primary medium of communication. Many linguists, however, found this approach too restrictive; they felt that generativists *should* look at a broader range of phenomena. The political atmosphere of the late 1960s and early 1970s further encouraged many serious students of language to adopt the generative semantic program, which by combining work on formal grammar with concern for the use of language in the real world promised to satisfy their intellectual interests as well as the demands of their social conscience. George Lakoff was undoubtedly correct when he wrote, "Nowadays students are interested in generative semantics because it is a way for them to investigate the nature of human thought and social interaction."[26]

The broadening of the scope of grammatical analysis, however, inevitably undermined the attempts to construct a formal theory; the broad questions with which generative semanticists concerned themselves simply defied statement in formal terms. For George Lakoff, the refusal to present formal statements was to become a matter of principle; he explicitly advocated the return to the practice of presenting informal, purely descriptive accounts of exotic languages.[27] And Robin Lakoff even argued for a shift away from formalism on explicitly feminist grounds:

> . . . many of those who have in the past been turned off by undue obeisance to formalism have been women. . . . I feel that it is the emphasis on formal description of the superficial aspects of language that many of us find discouraging: hence many women, in an attempt to escape into relevance, go into psycholinguistics and sociolinguistics . . . but are lost to the mainstream and often end up dissatisfied anyhow. I don't know, nor does anyone, whether there is an inherent indisposition toward formalism among women, or whether it is a learned trait that may eventually be overcome; I know merely that it is the case now and is apt to remain so for some time to come. I think it is criminal to attract people into a field and then waste their abilities and insult their intelligence by telling them there is no place for the talents they have there.[28]

Part of the initial success of the generative semanticists must be attributed to their wide-ranging sphere of influence. By the early 1970s, generative semanticists had radiated into teaching positions all over the United States, while almost all of Chomsky's followers were at MIT.

This not only gave generative semantics the aura of a national "movement," but it meant that ten times as many students were being taught generative semantics as were being taught the alternative. The "in-group" atmosphere that then characterized (and to a certain extent still characterizes) the MIT Linguistics Department contrasted sharply with the missionary zeal of the generative semanticists.

Even while generative semanticists disputed the narrow focus of Chomsky's theory, other critics expressed increasing dissatisfaction with Chomsky's claims about the innate basis of grammar. Alternative hypotheses were formulated which, it was hoped, could deal with the same range of facts without the need for the innate syntactic principles that many found jarring to common sense. The Swiss psychologist Jean Piaget's theories offered the most popular alternative. Piaget believed that general principles governing learning could account for linguistic development, thereby obviating any need for a concept such as universal grammar.[29] Piaget's theory of the acquisition of knowledge, "developmental constructivism," posited the existence of "regulatory or autoregulatory mechanisms" which come into play at each stage in the child's cognitive development. In principle, these mechanisms regulate the child's acquisition of classificatory abilities, means-end knowledge, symbolic play, and much else in addition to language. In the early 1970s, more and more psycholinguists abandoned Chomsky's conception of innate grammatical universals and turned to the Piagetian idea that language acquisition results from the interaction of all-purpose cognitive skills with external environmental stimuli.

As a result of the combined challenges of generative semantics and Piagetian psycholinguistics, the prestige of generative grammar fell to an all-time low around 1975. Since then, its relative importance within the field has gradually increased. Part of the renewed success of generative grammar must be attributed to the utter polarization and collapse of generative semantics by the late 1970s. On the one hand, those interested in the social context of language moved ever closer to sociolinguistics. The sociological orientation to language had never amounted to much in the United States before the late 1960s, when there was a true explosion of interest in the study of the social aspect of language. Certainly this was part of the appeal of generative semantics at the beginning. But more than a few students found their interest shifting away from grammar construction altogether and toward the new and fast-growing subdiscipline of sociolinguistics. Sociolinguists looked with amazement at the generative semanticist program of attempting to treat societal phenomena in a framework originally designed to handle such sentence-level properties as morpheme order and vowel alternations. They found no difficulty in convincing those generative semanticists most committed to studying language in its social context to drop whatever pretense they still might have of doing a grammatical analysis, and to approach the subject matter instead from the traditional perspective of the social sciences.

On the other hand, those interested in developing a theory capable of characterizing the strictly grammatical properties of human language drew back to the more traditional autonomous conception of generative grammar, which excludes societal facts from the grammar itself. They had come to feel that generative semanticists, by considering all linguistic facts as matter for grammatical analysis, had gotten too mired down in unanalyzed data to be able to develop any formal principles at all. Indeed, many papers in generative semantics consisted of little more than informal presentations of fascinating facts about language.

The collapse of generative semantics was followed closely by a series of important advances in the understanding of the properties of universal grammar. Chomsky's "Government-Binding Theory," introduced in 1979,[30] succeeded in unifying a number of disparate and seemingly recalcitrant grammatical phenomena into a conceptually simple and elegant overall framework of principles. This work has not only rekindled interest in formal grammar among American linguists, but has drawn to Chomsky for the first time a significant international following. Indeed, the Government-Binding Theory, which, incidentally, Chomsky first presented in a series of lectures in Pisa, Italy, has at least as many supporters outside the United States as inside.*

The computer revolution, too, has begun to boost generativist fortunes. Advances in both computer technology and the formal theory of grammar have made possible applications of the theory to practical tasks that were inconceivable twenty years ago. For example, in the last few years computer specialists, working with gener-

* With the exception of Great Britain, the Netherlands, Australia, and Japan, where in the 1970s some senior professors began to encourage the development of generativist-oriented programs, Chomsky's supporters outside of North America are mostly at the lowest rungs of the academic hierarchy.

ative grammarians, have written programs that process written English well enough to understand questions of some degree of complexity, to search for the answer to them in a computerized data base, and to respond in written English. The computer industry has invested millions in a new generation of "friendly" computers, and what could be a more "friendly" way to interact with a computer, as Colonel Gaines pointed out, than by giving it instructions in one's own native language? It stands to reason that those with the highest degree of the relevant technical knowledge of grammar, generative grammarians, should be looked on as a valuable resource by the industry. Indeed, IBM, Hewlett-Packard, and Xerox, among others, already have generativists on the payroll. There is every reason to think that the industry demand for their skills will escalate. While those committed to generativist principles are delighted that the applicability of those principles is being demonstrated in practice, and, of course, are pleased that the computer revolution is creating more job opportunities for trained linguists, they also see the danger that the needs of technology will significantly distort the nature of the research being carried out in the field. If, for example, a particular generativist framework most satisfactory in elucidating the nature of universal grammar is less suited than some other framework for computer applications, industry would naturally be more likely to support the latter than the former, thereby channeling research toward engineering applications and away from the development of the most linguistically and psychologically adequate theory. This has not happened yet, but many generativists see a real possibility that it might.

94

Still, whatever hope the future may hold, generative grammar is at present only moderately successful—far from the dominant position it enjoyed in the mid-sixties. MIT is consistently voted the leading American linguistics department,[31] and, incontestably, its graduates get what are seen as the best jobs. Generativist Ph.D.'s from other departments, however, fare no better in the job market than their nongenerativist competitors. The major granting agencies, such as the National Science Foundation and the American Council of Learned Societies, allot only a minority of their appropriations to generativists, though probably practitioners of expensive undertakings such as experimental phonetics and acquisition studies apply for the most. By no criteria imaginable do generativists hold sway over the organs of power in the field. Only two yearly elected presidents in the history of the Linguistic Society of America have been chosen from their ranks, and generativists make up a small percentage of the society's committee members. As far as *Language,* the journal sponsored by the society, is concerned, its editor is a nongenerativist and its editorial committee has only a bare majority of generative grammarians. The articles and reviews published in *Language* do not even reveal this degree of generativist strength; only about a third are oriented to generative grammar.

Although some linguists still claim that advocates of the generativist "paradigm" are powerful enough to "silence" critics lacking tenure in their universities,[32] Chomsky's critics, tenured or nontenured, have hardly been "silenced." No journal exists that does not regularly publish criticisms of his views, including *Linguistic Inquiry,* edited at Chomsky's home department at MIT.

At present, about a third of American linguists are either generative grammarians or presuppose generative grammar in their studies of first-language acquisition, second-language learning, or whatever; another third approach grammar from a nongenerativist direction or reject Chomskyan assumptions in their experimental or applied work; and the final third address aspects of language in which one's stand on such questions is unimportant, such as is the case in certain subareas of sociolinguistics and phonetics. And this breakdown does not take into account the many humanistically oriented language scholars who do not even identify themselves as linguists but work in literature departments instead.

What then of the much-vaunted "Chomskyan revolution"? Chomsky himself steadfastly denies the idea that the field has ever undergone one. After offering his opinion to an interviewer that "*if* the kind of linguistics I am interested in survives in the United States, it may very likely be in [cognitive science programs] rather than in linguistics departments,"[33] he goes on to say:

> At least as I look back over my own relation to the field, at every point it has been completely isolated, or almost completely isolated. I do not see that the situation is very different now. . . . But I cannot think of any time when the kind of work that I was doing was of any interest to any more than a very tiny fraction of people in the field.[34]

Chomsky's influence is enormous, but influence does not necessarily bring agreement. He undoubtedly commands the allegiance of more than "a tiny fraction" of the world's linguists, but if Chomsky is the most followed scholar in the field, he is also the most attacked. The precise figures are open to speculation, but one fact is clear: his ideas have thoroughly transformed linguistics. No student of language, from whatever orientation, can undertake serious linguistic research without taking them into account.

5

THE OPPOSITION

TO AUTONOMOUS LINGUISTICS

THE debates between Chomsky and his critics described in the last chapter basically all took place within the realm of autonomous grammar. Generative grammarians may have challenged the premises of structuralists, and may in turn have been challenged by generative semanticists, but the disputes never touched the essential assumptions of autonomous linguistics. However, alternative orientations have always existed parallel to autonomous linguistics, and often have defined themselves in opposition to it. Some have objected merely to the priorities set by those who would analyze language as an autonomous system, while others have challenged the very intellectual worth and political credibility of autonomous linguistics.

From its inception, autonomous linguistics provoked an elitist opposition from the direction of humanistic scholarship. First, the classical philologists and then scholars of Western literature scorned the attention paid by autonomous linguistics to nonliterary languages and the dialects of the common people. The opposition from the former was destined to fail along with the idea that every true gentleman deserves a classical education. As the languages of ancient Greece and Rome ceased to form the center of the academic curriculum, so too did the idea that these languages should form the basis for linguistic studies. Yet the legacy of the philologists' opposition lives on at those universities where the classical languages are still stressed. At Oxford and Cambridge, for example, autonomous linguistics of any variety has only a token presence. On the other hand, the elitist attitudes of some literary scholars continues to retard the development of structural linguistics and generative grammar. While their opposition was effective only temporarily in North America, even today in continental Europe proposals for structuralist-oriented programs are vetoed on the ground that they would detract from the study of the great literary languages.

But it would be a mistake to regard the humanistic opposition to autonomous linguistics as being tied necessarily to elitist sentiments. Quite the contrary, in fact: that opposition typically sees its view of language as embodying the essence of human freedom and the autonomous view as a threat to it. In particular, humanist critics object to what they see as the *depersonalization* of language implicit in the structuralists' inventories of grammatical elements and in the generativists' systems of rules. Probably the most articulate statement of this position is the late Paul Goodman's *Speaking and Language: Defense of Poetry*.[1] Goodman eloquently argued that the essence of the human creative spirit is the ability to transcend structures and rules, and that the grammarians' constructs, far from having any real significance, are nothing but the fetters of arbitrary convention. The true poet, Goodman believed, has no use for such constructs—and we are all potential poets. George Steiner's *After Babel: Aspects of Meaning and Translation* offers a similar view. As Steiner sees it, the "private self," the product of "human individuation," naturally rebels against sterile, mechanical rules. "To know more of language and translation," Steiner says, "we must pass from the 'deep structures' of transformational grammar to the deeper structures of the poet."[2]

Humanistic opponents of autonomous linguistics particularly single out for attack the *langue-parole* (and competence-performance) dichotomies. For example, Roy Harris, in his book *The Language Makers*,[3] sees nothing in *langue* but "collective uniformity." Since *langue* is the common property of all speakers of a particular language, it is a device for subordinating the will of the individual to that of the community as a whole. The homogenization implied by Chomsky's "universal grammar" has grave consequences for all of culture. As Ian Robinson has put it:

> In the end it must be a kind of philistinism in a linguist to think, as Chomsky does with his doctrine of

universals, of all languages as pretty much alike. It means that he has lost that wonder at the splendid multiplicity of language and languages which is the other side of the wondering at language as a common human possession. Chomsky's semantic universals are as if a critic were to try to explain great poems (as is not unknown) by looking for an underlying Great Poetry that they share. To do so would inevitably be to have lost interest in poems, as well as in the possibility of discussing poetry in general.[4]

What is the alternative task for the linguist, then? Robinson writes: "I don't believe it would do the subject any harm if linguists were to meditate upon particular pieces of language for a decade or two, instead [of looking for rules and universals] — they could read a few poems, for instance."[5]

The impact of the humanistic critique in the United States has been diminished by the fact that its practitioners have left the field of linguistics or have been excluded from it altogether. Since they are seen as literary, rather than linguistic, scholars, the field has found it easy to ignore them.* I doubt that more than a dozen autonomous linguists in the past thirty years have responded to any criticism of their ideas that is based on an appeal to humanistic sensibilities.[6]

On the other hand, the critique of autonomous linguistics from the opposite direction — the sociological orientation — has had a greater, more sustained influence.

* The conflict between humanistic scholars and their opponents is still being intensely fought out in English departments, however, where the principal adversary for the former is not generative grammar but rather the European structuralist movement, i.e., Saussure as delivered through (especially) Barthes, Derrida, and Lacan.

Many who approach language from a sociological vantage point reject the premise that any aspect of a language should be analyzed independently of the society in which that language is spoken. That such a practice might be fruitful is simply regarded as inconceivable by many in the field. Indeed, autonomous linguistics seems to offend the common sense. Anyone who has taught an introductory linguistics class knows that many of the brightest students at first simply assume that the structure of the society dictates the structure of the language; indeed, for some, the primary motivation for taking the class is the desire to learn more precisely the nature of the society-language link.

The most coherent expression of the idea that language structure is intimately related to the external world of its speakers has evolved in the tradition of Marxist writings about language. Although neither Marx nor Engels ever presented a developed theory of language, paragraphs here and there throughout their writings offer clues to their ideas on this topic. There is no avoiding the conclusion that what they say is in part self-contradictory. This is hardly surprising: the thinking of Marx and Engels evolved considerably over their long careers, and, in any event, there is no reason why consistency should emerge on a topic that was of little immediate concern to them. There is one passage, however, that seems unambiguous in its meaning, and it is the one most commonly cited by twentieth-century Marxist linguists. In *The German Ideology*, Marx and Engels write:

> Language is as old as consciousness, language *is* practical consciousness that exists also for other men, and for that reason alone it really exists for me

personally as well; language, like consciousness, only arises from the need, the necessity, of intercourse with other men. Where there exists a relationship, it exists for me: the animal does not enter into any relation at all. For the animal, its relation to others does not exist as a relation. Consciousness is, therefore, from the very beginning a social product, and remains so as long as men exist at all.[7]

Consciousness is a social product; language is (practical) consciousness; therefore language is a social product. The syllogism could not be more straightforward; in this passage, Marx and Engels clearly present language as a superstructural phenomenon, i.e., one that is influenced by—and in turn influences, —the economic base of the society. And how would a Marxist undertake the study of language, given such a conclusion? The same way one would undertake the study of other superstructural phenomena, such as cultural institutions or ideology: through a detailed examination of the interacting economic and historical factors that contribute to its organization and use. Autonomous linguistics, given such a conclusion, would be as unthinkable as autonomous jurisprudence.

The first explicitly Marxist linguistic study, the Russian V. N. Vološinov's *Marxism and the Philosophy of Language,* was written in the late 1920s.[8] Vološinov directed his attention to the stylistic aspect of language, analyzing the different forms an utterance can take. He demonstrated that the devices used to portray particular forms such as reported speech (speech used to recount that of others), direct discourse, and indirect discourse could be linked historically to the structure of the society at the time of writing. For example, Vološinov argued that the move from a strictly linear prose style to a more pictorial one between medieval and Renaissance France reflected a move away from authoritarianism and dogmatism, which he attributed to the changing class structure of French society.

Since Vološinov's study, Marxist linguistics has carried its investigation into every area of contact between language and society. Thus, a typical paper might investigate the manner in which language imposes the precepts of the dominant group on the larger society. Another might document the difference between working-class and middle-class speech in some urban center. Another might cite historical examples of the language of a conquering power remaining the ruling-class speech long after the conquest, as did Norman French in England for over two centuries after 1066. Another might argue that the movement for an "international language," such as Esperanto, is tied to specific class interests. And another might defend the claim that the disparity is extreme between the ideology of linguistic harmony in Switzerland and other countries and the actual situation.

Moreover, a great many papers in the tradition of Marxist linguistics stress the unity of theory and practice so central to Marxist thinking, and attempt to go beyond the mere description of language-class linkages. It is not uncommon for a paper, say, on the speech of Turkish workers in Berlin or Hamburg, after documenting how their oppression is heightened by their language differences from the German majority, to call for the implementation of specific reforms to help alleviate the situation. Others go even farther: they treat the specific language situation as emblematic of the class structure of the entire society, and outline how the Turks' struggle for linguistic equality can form part of a general movement for revolutionary change.

Given the differences between the research program of autonomous linguistics and that of Marxist scholarship, it is not surprising that there are very few individuals whose writings about language represent a contribution to both.* One such individual is Joseph Emonds, who was trained in linguistics at MIT. In a recent study of English subject pronouns, Emonds proposed a set of generative rules to account for their grammatical properties and described the social circumstances governing their use.[9] Emonds argues that in sentences with conjoined subject pronouns, the prescription of nominative pronouns (*he and I left*) instead of objective pronouns (*him and me left*) is an example of a linguistic barrier consciously imposed by the dominant socioeconomic class to separate itself from the majority. Emonds provides evidence from the principles of universal grammar, from the history of the construction, and from an observation of the acquisition and use of subject pronouns by children that the nominative forms would disappear practically overnight if the advocacy of their use did not serve as a linguistic obstacle to disenfranchised sections of the population.

Despite the work of Emonds and a few others, it seems

* There are, however, numerous generative grammarians who identify themselves as Marxists but whose academic research priorities do not include the study of language in its social context.

fair to say that most Marxist students of language regard autonomous linguistics with feelings ranging from disinterest to outright hostility. For many Marxists, the grammar-writing activity of autonomous linguists seems no worse than a mere distraction from the important study of the social reality of language. But others have concluded that autonomous linguistics is literally incompatible with Marxism. As they see it, language is a superstructural phenomenon not just in its social and cultural aspect but rather in *all* its manifestations, including the grammatical. Vološinov himself held this point of view. He saw Saussure's structuralism as "abstract objectivism," an ahistorical closed system, incompatible with the true nature of language, which is rather a "ceaseless flow of becoming."[10] He also condemned structuralism for failing to recognize language in its components and structure as an instrument of ideology, and considered this "divorce of language from its ideological impletion . . . one of abstract objectivism's most serious errors."[11]

For Vološinov, the pure grammatical studies favored by autonomous linguistics should be replaced by efforts to elucidate how the word reflects the interrelationship of base and superstructure, i.e., "how actual existence (the basis) determines sign and how sign reflects and refracts existence in its process of generation."[12] The roots of the relationship between sign and existence are to be found, of course, outside of language itself: "Production relations and the sociopolitical order shaped by those relations determine the full range of verbal contacts between people, all the forms and means of their verbal communication — at work, in political life, in ideological creativity. In turn, from the conditions, forms, and types of verbal communication derive not only the forms but also the themes of speech performances."[13]

The work of two American linguists active between the two world wars, Edward Sapir and Benjamin Whorf, lent important support to the idea of an intimate linkage between language structure and "external" phenomena. Sapir believed that the structure of one's language directly shapes one's view of the world, and that different structures impose on the consciousness a different perception of reality:

> Language . . . actually defines experience for us by reason of its formal completeness and because of our unconscious projection of its implicit expectations into the field of experience. . . . Such categories as number, gender, case, tense . . . are not so much discovered in experience as imposed upon it because of the tyrannical hold that linguistic form has upon our orientation in the world.[14]

Sapir's ideas were further developed and applied to specific languages by his student Whorf. Since the 1940s, the notion that linguistic structure is a determinant of worldview has been known as the "Sapir-Whorf hypothesis."

Whorf based his ideas about language-culture interconnections on his study of various American Indian tribes, especially the Hopi. For example, Whorf observed that the Hopi have "no general notion or intuition of TIME as a smooth flowing continuum in which everything in the universe proceeds at an equal rate, out of a future, through a present, into a past; or, in which, to reverse the picture, the observer is being carried in the stream of duration continuously away from a past and into a future."[15] Whorf related this "absence" to Hopi linguistic structure:

> The Hopi language is seen to contain no words, grammatical forms, constructions or expressions that refer directly to what we call "time," or to past, present, or future, or to enduring or lasting, or to motion as kinematic rather than dynamic (i.e. as a continuous translation in space and time rather than as an exhibition of dynamic effort in a certain process), or that even refer to space in such a way as to exclude that element of extension or existence that we call "time," and so by implication leave a residue that could be referred to as "time." Hence, the Hopi language contains no reference to "time," either explicit or implicit.[16]

In short, "the Hopi language and culture conceal a metaphysics."[17]

The Sapir-Whorf hypothesis never initiated a significant research program among American linguists (though there was a flurry of interest in it in the 1950s). The commitment of most of the major figures in the field to autonomy led them to view it with skepticism; only those with more "anthropological" interests devoted much time to exploring its possibilities. But in Europe, where the commitment to autonomous linguistics was relatively weak, and that to Marxism relatively strong, the hypothesis was received enthusiastically and reinterpreted along Marxist lines.[18] Where Sapir and Whorf saw grammatical structure as the determinant of a people's worldview, the Europeans have attempted to ground grammatical structure *as well as* worldview in social class and conceptions ultimately based on it.

Contemporary Marxist linguistic scholars frequently cite work in the Whorfian tradition in order to demonstrate the superstructural nature of grammar. And the evidence they adduce for such an idea derives from studies of Western culture as well. As sociolinguistic research has revealed, people who belong to different social classes invariably have forms of speech that differ in some structural property or they speak different languages altogether.

Max K. Adler, the West German Marxist linguist, argues:

> When it comes to the class structure of language, a Marxist should be bound to accept [this idea]. . . . There is at least some evidence that the working class speaks differently from the middle and upper classes, and there are also differences between middle-class and upper-class speech. . . . We have only to look at one glaring example. For some years American linguists investigated what they called "Black English." In fact, this language is confined to the Negro poor in the United States. As soon as a black man in America climbs up the social ladder and becomes middle class he changes from "Black" English to the educated form of American English. . . . The differences between working-class and middle- and upper-class speech occurs in every capitalist society; how far these two forms of a language differ from each other depends mainly on the strength of the antagonism between the classes in the particular society.[19]

Adler and his fellow Marxist critics of autonomous linguistics deduce the superstructural nature of grammar from the existence of class dialects and their putative relationship to class antagonisms, from the fact that in every society certain words and expressions are common to members of particular classes, and from a host of other correlations between grammar and social class. In their view, any theory that sees linguistic structure as in some fundamental way autonomous, or transcending class (and thus suggesting a linguistic practice that sidesteps societal divisions) is by definition a product of bourgeois ideology. Such Marxists see Chomsky in particular as nothing but the latest in a long procession of intellectuals who, by relegating social class to a peripheral position, objectively serve ruling-class interests.

Many contemporary Marxist linguists also object to autonomy for its factoring out of *langue* from *parole* and its concomitant "objectification" as an inventory of grammatical elements or set of generative rules. For example, Raymond Williams, in *Marxism and Literature*, while acknowledging the "remarkable results" of structuralist assumptions in linguistics, dismisses structuralism nevertheless as "the final reinforcement of a concept of language as an (alien) objective system."[20] As Williams sees it, the "objectification" of abstract structure places language outside the historical and social process. It is the task for Marxists to notice

> first, that history, in its most specific, active, and connecting senses, has disappeared . . . from this [structuralist] account of so central a social activity as language; and second that the categories in which this version of system has been developed are the

familiar bourgeois categories in which an abstract separation and distinction between the "individual" and the "social" have become so habitual that they are taken as "natural" starting points.[21]

David Silverman and Brian Torode, in *The Material Word*, go even further than *Marxism and Literature*, implying that the concepts of "deep structure" and related abstractions found in generative grammar are rooted in some notion of supranatural transcendence:

> [The language-speech distinction] implies that what speech shows is an unseen and unseeable element which animates it. Whether formulated as God, deep structure (structuralism, Chomsky), Being or a capitalized Language (Heidegger), these transcendental realities are accorded the respect denied to them by those who would treat speech as a purely technical instrument. Recognizing the relation between speech and language as one between man and the gods, the paramount aim has become to avoid angering the gods by pretending to be one.[22]

Given this direction in modern Marxist thinking about language, it is hardly surprising that the success of generative grammar in any country has been inversely proportional to the depth of tradition of Marxist scholarship there. In West Germany, for example, where Marxist tradition is very strong, generative grammar has almost no presence.

But it is the Soviet Union that offers the most dramatic example of the adventures of Marxist linguistics and its conflicts with autonomy. In the late 1920s, the banner of

"Marxist linguistics" was taken up in the Soviet Union by a half-Scottish, half-Georgian researcher on the Caucasian languages named Nikolaj Jakovlevič Marr. By the time of Marr's death in 1934, his ideas already dominated Soviet linguistics, a position they held until Stalin's personal intervention in 1950.[23]

Marr's fully developed theory, "stadialism," argued that economic revolutions (in the Marxist sense) produce linguistic revolutions. In other words, language is conceived of as superstructural in the most mechanical sense possible—there are literally "feudal languages," "capitalist languages," "socialist languages," and so on. Moreover, every conceivable aspect of language is a superstructural phenomenon, down to the most minute phonetic detail.

Since societies differ in terms of their stage of development, it follows that languages must as well. Marr attempted to identify the linguistic stages by morphological characteristics, such as the complexity of inflectional endings. Languages more "primitive" morphologically, such as Chinese, he assigned to an earlier rung of development than the more morphologically complex, such as the Indo-European and Semitic languages. He further attempted to correlate each linguistic stage with a stage of social development—no easy task, since the "highest" linguistic stage turns out to contain both the languages of Ethiopian tribespeople and Russian, the language of a "socialist" society. Naturally, the idea that all languages were class languages had to be accompanied by the idea that there could not be such a thing as a *national* language. Indeed, Marr went so far as to claim that the speech of the typical French worker has more in common with that of the typical German worker than it does with that of a French capitalist.

In spite of such peculiar ideas, no linguistics opposed to his views was acceptable in the Soviet Union until 1950. All varieties of structuralism were officially outlawed. As late as 1949 the Presidium of the USSR Academy of Sciences endorsed his theories, labeling comparative and formal linguistics "bourgeois," "reactionary," "racist," and "justifying an imperialist foreign policy."[24]

But by then a storm was brewing. Whatever Soviet ideology might have dictated, the nation's linguists *could not* put Marr's ideas into practice. As one observer of the 1949 meeting noted: "The work of the session revealed the generally unsatisfactory situation in the field of linguistics." He went on to add: "The [N. Ja. Marr] Institute of Language and Thought was unable to present a single report throwing light on the basic questions of Marr's teaching." Indeed, no linguists in the field of the Russian language took part in the work of the session.[25]

The disaffected linguists, frustrated by their own inability to carry out reasonable research and embarrassed at the international ridicule to which Soviet linguistics was being subjected, sought aid in the highest quarter of the land—they went to Stalin. And Stalin intervened for them personally, on their behalf. On May 9, 1950, noting "the unsatisfactory state of Soviet linguistics," the newspaper *Pravda* launched an "open discussion" on linguistic matters.[26] Fourteen short articles followed in the next six weeks, some pro-Marr and some anti. On June 20, Stalin contributed a piece thoroughly hostile to the Marrist approach. The following two weeks saw sixteen new pieces, including a few more by Stalin, and all endorsing Stalin's position. One contributor noted that the problem had now been resolved "in wise Stalinist fashion";[27] another that "a new era in the history of Soviet linguistics"[28] had been initiated; another hailed Stalin's piece as "a cause for celebration," and promised "to correct my errors honestly in future work";[29] and so on. On July 4, the debate was officially closed. The Marrist period in Soviet linguistics had come to an end.

What Stalin did was no less than to assert the autonomy of grammar. While his words would hardly have raised an eyebrow in any Western linguistics journal, it was the first time since the 1920s that such sentiments had been expressed openly in Russia:

> Grammar is the outcome of a prolonged work of abstraction of human thought; it is a gauge of the tremendous achievement of thought. . . . In this respect grammar resembles geometry, which creates its laws by a process of abstraction from concrete objects, regarding objects as bodies without any concreteness, and defining the relations between them, not as the concrete relations of concrete objects, but as the relations of bodies in general, without any concreteness.[30]

If grammar is like abstract geometry in the brain, then it could hardly be a superstructural phenomenon. And Stalin provided a number of arguments that it is not one. For example, the Russian Revolution completely altered the political and legal institutions of Russian society, yet "the Russian language has remained essentially what it was before."[31] Only marginal areas of the vocabulary had undergone a change.

What really motivated Stalin to intervene? It is hard to believe that in the closing years of his life he had actually come to take a personal interest in some minor academic specialty or that the state of Soviet linguistics in the eyes of Western scholars was a matter of genuine concern to him. What necessitated the destruction of Marr's ideas was that they were *antinationalist* ideas. By the 1940s the Soviet Union had embarked on an ultranationalistic course. World War II was labeled the "Great Patriotic War" to defend the Russian Fatherland. Patriotic songs and slogans were reintroduced. And after the war, the ravaged population was encouraged in nationalistic terms to rebuild its homeland, with the rhetoric of socialism downplayed to the fullest extent possible. Soviet scholars in this period participated in the reconstruction of a national culture, rediscovering the greatness, wealth, and beauty of the Russian language, not incidentally a force that could serve to unify a majority of the Soviet people.

The last thing Stalin wanted was a linguistic theory that downplayed the importance of Russian. Marr's ideas fell from favor not because he believed that grammar was superstructural but because his rejection of the possibility of national languages struck at Stalin's immediate goal for the increased predominance of Russian.[32]

The change in orientation of Soviet linguistics after the fall of Marrism was less dramatic than one might suppose. True, the administrators of the various organizations concerned with linguistics were replaced by those who had sought Stalin's aid against Marr, but no great torrent of structural linguistics was unleashed. The immediate effect was to produce a considerable amount of research in traditional comparative linguistics, which was now labeled "Marxist." It was (re)discovered that Engels had not only commented favorably in his *Anti-Dühring* on the work of the comparativists Bopp, Grimm, and Dietz but had even considered himself an amateur comparative linguist. More importantly for the debate with Marrism, Engels had dismissed entirely the possibility of tying phonological change to a change in the economic base of society, writing, "It will hardly be possible for anybody, without being ridiculous . . . to explain the economic origin of High German vocalic changes which divide Germany [in dialect matters] into two halves." Indeed, opponents of Marr's theories pointed out that Engels, despite his and Marx's remarks in *The German Ideology*, later came to regard language more as an instrument of production (i.e., a tool) than as a superstructural phenomenon. And they cited a passage from Marx's "Introduction to a Critique of Political Economy" that seemed implicitly to endorse autonomous linguistics by referring to the "laws and categories" that all languages have "in common."[33]

Structural linguistics started making headway in the Soviet Union only in the very late 1950s, largely in response to the needs of machine translation. Most of the early defenses of structuralism pointed to the necessity of formal description of language as a prerequisite to automatic language-data processing. However, the opposition to structural approaches continued to maintain its hold on language and linguistics programs. Throughout the 1970s, a loose coalition of comparativists, descriptive linguists of a traditional sort, and some residual Marrists reasserted their power. And they were successful. The two leading Soviet structuralists, I. A. Melčuk and S. K. Šaumjan, found it more advisable to emigrate to North America than to wage a losing battle against their professional opponents. The final blow was struck in 1983, with the retirement of V. A. Zvegincev, the head of the Department of Structural and Applied Linguistics at the University of Moscow. The authorities used the opportunity to close down his department—where a considerable amount of structuralist theorizing took place—and merge it into the more traditionally oriented Department of General Linguistics. There is little work now being done on formal approaches to grammar in the Soviet Union outside of the computer industry, which, of course, is not part of the system of higher education.

The situation in the U.S. is, of course, the reverse. Here the "traditional" emphasis has been on autonomy, and the only significant ongoing Marxist linguistic research has been in stylistics and discourse analysis, and is carried out exclusively in literature rather than linguistics departments. Although the impact of the Marxist critique has been felt by autonomous linguists here, there has been no move to apply Marxist assumptions to grammatical studies. Virtually all such work, to the extent that it is explicitly Marxist, is still carried on outside of North America. This is not to say that there is no sociologically oriented opposition to autonomy here. Far from it. Rather, the opposition has taken a different form. Many American sociolinguists denigrate autonomous linguistics (which, in practice, means that they denigrate generative grammar) not so much for its content as for its emphasis. They object on "moral" grounds, so to speak. While in principle they may accept the generativist conception of an autonomously functioning mental grammar, they feel that to devote one's time to constructing such a grammar is to forsake one's political and ethical responsibilities. With language differences the seeming cause of so many social problems, from riots in Belgium to the bad performance of minority students in the American public schools, the advocates of this position ask how anyone with a social conscience could spend time formulating abstract—and abstracted—grammatical rules. Rather, one's priorities should be directed to placing one's expertise at the disposal of those who can most benefit from it.

The linguist Dell Hymes has been the moral critique's most articulate spokesperson. Typically, Hymes has no principled disagreement with the essentials of Chomsky's theory; indeed, he has endorsed it in glowing terms: "Chomsky's type of explanatory adequacy leads away from speech, and from languages, to relationships possibly universal to all languages, and possibly inherent in human nature. It is an exciting and worthwhile prospect."[34] The problem, as Hymes sees it, is not that Chomsky's theory is wrong; it is that Chomsky has proposed the wrong theory. What he *should* be doing is sociolinguistics. Since Chomsky, of all linguists, is most able to analyze the linguistic dimension of "the social realities of language,"[35] he does a social disservice by confining his work to the elaboration of autonomous grammatical theory.

If Chomsky and his supporters had happened to have right-wing political views or even be apolitical, their lack of interest in the "social realities of language" would be understandable to Hymes. But what especially disturbs him is that in all respects but linguistic ones they share his politics: "Many participants in formal linguistics are liberal or radical in social views, and yet their methodological commitments prevent them from dealing with the verbal part of the problems of the communities of concern to them."[36]

Hymes's critique has been echoed throughout the sociolinguistic community. Thus Hartmut Haberland and Jacob L. Mey, founders of a journal devoted to the problems of language use rather than structure, insist on the contradiction and irrelevance of a linguistics that sets itself apart from politics:

> Many linguists deeply regret that they have to earn their living by a science that can be used for the construction of military information systems, psychological warfare, counterinsurgency strategies, and the like. They dedicate their books to "the children of Vietnam," or make up a few anti-imperialistic sentences as examples. But there is not much help in such a practice: a linguistics that pretends to be "emancipatory," while going about its strictly linguistic business as usual, has little to contribute to what we consider a worthwhile pragmatics.[37]

Feminist writers on language have joined the attack, and for analogous reasons. Chomsky's theoretical orientation seems irrelevant and insensitive to the oppression of women, and at odds with the feminist enterprise, "for feminism above all proposes cultural, and linguistics individual, descriptions of grammars and explanations of the speaker's understanding of these grammars."[38]

The idea that there might be anything politically progressive in Chomsky's notion of an innate universal grammar, the common possession of all humans, carries little weight: "No theorist of apartheid is likely to be daunted by being reminded that the African child can effortlessly acquire Xhosa—or, come to that, Afrikaans."[39] Again, the implication is clear: linguists who put their politics where their mouth is will abandon generative grammar and turn to language in its social context.

The academic study of language in society began in the United States in the postwar years and reached its high point in the liberal climate of the sixties and seventies. Its concerns have always been intimately tied to social developments here and abroad. For example, the American black movement of the sixties coincided with a rush of investigations into the speech of urban minorities, particularly ghetto blacks. Research on black language has ranged from detailed technical analyses of its grammatical properties to studies of the effects that speaking it have on the educational level of black schoolchildren. Or, to take another example, the field of national language planning came into being in response to certain problems faced by the newly independent countries of the Third World. In such countries, virtually all of which are multilingual, decisions had to be arrived at practically overnight on what the official national language(s) would be, what role would be accorded to regional languages, in what language(s) education would take place, etc. It is the task of national language planners to study the existing language situation and to propose solutions, in some cases at the behest of the government itself. The literature of national language planning is now enormous, covering the situation from Papua New Guinea to Norway and analyzing the successes, as in Indonesia, and the failures, as in India.

The concerns of the women's movement have also been taken up by academic sociolinguistics. Numerous articles and books in the last fifteen years have considered how the status of women is reflected (and reinforced) by properties of language, and how the speech of women differs from that of men.

There are dozens of other subareas of sociolinguistics, including the ethnography of speaking, bilingualism research, and dialectology. The contents of a recent issue of *Language in Society* (December 1982), the leading American sociolinguistics journal, give a sense of the broad scope of the field. Topics include methods for studying social variation in Viennese German speech; a study of the social structure and peer terminology in a black adolescent gang; an investigation of the social and geographical determinants of the use of the expressions "dragonfly," "darning needle," or "diamond needle" for a particular species of insect by suburban New Yorkers; and a biographical sketch of the early twentieth-century linguist Hugo Schuchardt, whose work laid the basis for modern studies of pidgin and creole languages.*

Certainly the remarkable explosion of sociolinguistics in the mid-1960s was due in part to the federal government's increased support for academic research projects,

---

* Pidgin and creole languages are those that result from the contact of one language with another, normally a language of a colonial power with an indigenous language. Thus their study is of great interest to sociolinguists.

particularly those directed to "disadvantaged" sections of the population. Sociolinguistics received more than its share of this funding, most of it from agencies of the Department of Health, Education and Welfare. In fact, an examination of the public records shows that far more HEW money in the late 1960s and through the 1970s went to support sociolinguistics than generative grammar. Even the National Science Foundation (an independent governmental agency), which in the public mind is usually associated with highly technological projects, allocated more of its grant money to the former than to the latter. Likewise, private granting agencies—in particular, the Ford Foundation—have been generous in their support of sociolinguistic research. While in recent years, as one might expect, the absolute amount of money such research receives from granting agencies has declined, the relative level of governmental and foundation support for sociolinguistics continues to be high, exceeded only by funding of experimental work in phonetics, psycholinguistics, and neurolinguistics.*

While there is no "precise" way to measure the success of the sociolinguists' critique of autonomous linguistics, my impression is that it has been very effective indeed. Without question, the sociolinguists' moral appeal was to a considerable degree responsible for the eclipse of gen-

---

* Both the telephone and the computer industries have sponsored work in experimental phonetics, which more than any other branch of linguistics has produced immediately applicable results—the speech synthesis devices used in talking cash registers and video games are examples. Psycholinguistic and neurolinguistic research is sponsored in part for its potential application to the treatment of speech and learning disorders.

erative grammar in the 1970s. Indeed, it is not out of the question that the slow reemergence of interest in generative grammar in the past half dozen years is to some degree, however slight, correlated with the well-documented dulling of the American social conscience.

6

SOME THOUGHTS ON

THE AUTONOMY CONTROVERSY

A S WE have seen, the controversy over the value of
the autonomous orientation has been long and bitter, and shows no sign of resolution. On the one hand,
humanist intellectuals object to its failure to embody a
system of aesthetic standards; on the other, Marxists see
its much vaunted claim of "scientific neutrality" as nothing but a cover for an implicit support for the status quo,
while moralist sociolinguists deplore its irrelevance to the
important contemporary social concerns. The rifts are evident throughout the profession in North America: autonomous linguists have succeeded in excluding the
humanistic orientation from the field altogether, and

only a very few departments and journals grant equal representation to autonomous and sociological linguistics.

There are three reasons why autonomy has generated such vehement controversy. First, the very conception of an autonomous linguistics is quite threatening. To the humanist, who considers language our most intimate possession — the medium through which our humanity is manifested — the idea that language, or some central portion of it, might be isolable and capable of reification as an autonomous structural system poses a profound challenge. To those preoccupied with language as the medium for all socializing experience, the idea that at the core of language lies a *langue*, or competence, immune to social forces, is equally disturbing.

Moreover, the exclusionary stance that many generativists — and in particular Chomsky — have taken toward the other orientations has only intensified the conflict. Chomsky has repeatedly conveyed the impression that not to do linguistics his way is not to do linguistics at all. For example, many of his writings begin with the statement that linguistics is a "branch of cognitive psychology."[1] Given such a definition, there is no way that sociolinguistics can be part of linguistics. Chomsky's understanding of "performance" is equally absolute. After defining "performance" as "the actual use of language in concrete situations,"[2] Chomsky writes that "the only studies of performance, outside of phonetics . . . are those carried out as a by-product of work in generative grammar."[3] Dell Hymes's reaction to this assertion expresses the sociological and humanistic opposition:

However, if (outside phonetics) only by-products of generative grammar qualify as studies of performance, what is to be said of more than two thousand years of rhetoric and poetics, and of investigations of the use of language in social interaction and cultural behavior? If these investigations are not performance, then the equation of performance with use of language has reduced the notion of "use" so much as to exclude most aspects of speaking. If these investigations *do* deal with performance subject-matter, then the term "study" is oddly restricted to just those investigations that arise as generative grammar by-products.[4]

Finally, autonomous linguistics is particularly controversial because it considers itself the only scientific approach. Generative grammar has only exacerbated the conflict by claiming an even greater scientific validity than empiricist structuralism, and asserting its right to a respect previously reserved for the natural sciences. As a theory governing a human domain that embodies complex, abstract, and putatively scientific principles, generative grammar demands to be taken seriously. But to the many who believe that the humanities and social sciences are inherently not susceptible to scientific methods, the possibility that autonomy, and especially generative theory, could be correct is very unsettling.

The field of linguistics has by now become so polarized that it is difficult to imagine it differently. And yet it is possible to believe in the intrinsic value of the principles of generative grammar without accepting the exclusionary stance that so many of its practitioners have taken.

In truth, humanistic linguists have very little reason to feel threatened by generative grammar. The two approaches touch on utterly different aspects of language. The generativists' model of grammatical competence characterizes the structures available for sentence formation and attempts to specify which are universal and which are language particular. But it makes no claim whatsoever about which of those structures one might actually use in performing an act of speaking, and says nothing at all about the aesthetic impact that such a speech act might have. The generativist is no more qualified to pass judgment on such matters than the crystallographer is qualified to design (or appraise) a diamond tiara.

To take another analogy, there are branches of cognitive psychology devoted to the question of how the human mind, in interaction with the eye and ear, imposes structure on visual or aural space. But nobody expects such areas of inquiry to explain what we choose to look at or listen to, or what aesthetic sensations we may receive by doing so. Likewise, it seems unreasonable to expect that the generativist could contribute much to the understanding of the aesthetics of creative language, or, conversely, that the student of poetics could have much to say about the structural relations that comprise linguistic competence.

But there is no reason not to call the concerns of both formal grammar and poetics "linguistic." Humanistic and autonomous linguistics each have their own distinct domains of inquiry, methodology, and goals, and each contribute in their own special way to an understanding of the totality of language. The field of linguistics certainly has enough room to embrace both orientations.

The same is true for the conflict between autonomous linguistics and the sociological perspective. Generativists study the form of language, not its content. The material conditions that determine what one might choose to speak at a particular time and place are simply beyond the scope of generativist theory. While the generativist believes that one draws on one's internalized grammatical competence when producing a sentence, the actual choice of the "message" is a matter for the social psychologist to investigate, not the grammarian.

Many who share the sociological orientation, however, reject the idea that it is possible to separate the form of language from its content. As we have seen, the dominant trend in Marxist linguistics, for example, firmly refuses to leave the study of grammatical form to the generativist. As many Marxists see it, even the grammatical aspect of language is superstructural; and thus, isolated studies of linguistic form are thoroughly misguided.

There is strong evidence, however, that grammar does lie outside the superstructure. Let us consider precisely what we would expect if it *were* a superstructural phenomenon. For one thing, we would expect the social divisions in a particular society to be reflected by forms of speech that differ in their structural properties. And, indeed, as we saw in the preceding chapter, there is such a reflection: grammatical differences correlate with class differences.

However, we would expect even more than this: we

would expect that whatever correlations exist between grammar and class not be coincidental. But such correlations *are* coincidental. Consider for purposes of comparison two phenomena that are undeniably superstructural: a society's dominant ideology and its prevalent religious belief. Both are connected in an intrinsic (though obviously not mechnical) fashion to productive relations; it is unthinkable, for example, that an ideology of survival of the fittest or a religious ethic of the individualistic Protestant sort could predominate in a feudal society. When we look at grammatical structure, on the other hand, a very different picture emerges. The matching of different types of grammatical structures against different types of social structures reveals no general correlative trends whatsoever. Any grammatical property can be found in the speech of members of any social class and at any known stage in human history. Grammatical structure is thus, in the Marxist sense, an *ahistorical* phenomenon.

Some examples might be useful in support of this (perhaps surprising) claim. Take, for example, negative concord (popularly "double negatives") in English, as in the sentence: *I don't know nothing about nobody.* The use of negative concord is almost exclusively restricted to the working class. For middle-class and upper-class speakers, only one negative element per simple sentence is possible: *I don't know anything about anybody.* The dialect without negative concord is considered the "standard." It is taught in the schools, used in the media, and, most obviously, it is the dialect of English speakers with power and privilege. Do these class-related facts about negative concord, then, support the idea that grammar is part of the superstructure? Not at all, for a rather fundamental reason: there is nothing intrinsic to working-class life that would lead a worker to prefer negative concord and a capitalist to avoid it. The correlation is a historical accident, and, as such, Marxist theory has nothing whatever to say about it. If the correlation were not accidental, then we would expect negative concord to occur disproportionately among the world's proletarians. But it is only in the English speech community that the correlation exists. All classes of Spanish speakers have concord; as far as this grammatical phenomenon is concerned, King Juan Carlos of Spain has more in common with a West Virginia coal miner than he does with President Reagan.

Many other examples prove the same point. In New York City, not pronouncing the "r" in words like *parka* and *father* is becoming more and more a unique feature of working-class speech: the middle class now generally pronounces the "r." Is there a natural connection between the life that New York workers endure and their r-less speech? No. In the south of England and in the old port cities of the American South, the facts are reversed. There it is r-fulness that is stigmatized and identified with the working class; upper-class speech contains no trace of the "r." Or consider the Black English feature of not pronouncing many word-final orthographic consonants (*find* pronounced "fine," *bold* pronounced "bol," and so on). Surely one would think that material factors are at the root of *that*. But all it takes is a look at standard, educated, Parisian French to disabuse oneself of such an idea. As this dialect developed from Latin, many final consonants were "dropped" from pronunciation—indeed this process is today far more advanced than it is in

Black English. And there was a period in which those French dialects in which consonant dropping was less advanced than in Parisian were stigmatized and identified as speech characteristics of the lower class. These grammatical and phonetic properties of a language demand an analysis on their *own* terms, not on those of a Marxist (or any other) theory of society. The existence of class dialects poses no challenge to autonomous linguistics.

The only subpart of a language's grammatical system that clearly to any significant extent depends on the objective conditions of life is vocabulary. Eskimos (and skiers!) do have more words for snow than Bedouin nomads, to give a hackneyed example. But even here, material need is only very indirectly related to the words one has at one's disposal. There is no objective reason why German speakers (from whatever social class) "need" three different words for *the* in the nominative singular and the whole baroque apparatus of grammatical gender that goes with them. And it is easy to think of concepts for which no word exists, despite the fact that it would be useful to have one. A common introductory linguistics class example is the nonexistence of a word to refer to a person one is both living with and romantically involved with, but not married to. Vocabulary is the most rapidly changing part of language, but, even so, it does not change fast enough to keep up with changing external conditions. So in Swedish, for example, one cannot simply say "uncle" or "aunt" — one must specify whether the relative is on the father's side or on the mother's. No doubt such a distinction was vital in primitive Scandinavian culture with its elaborate social distinctions based on nuances of kinship. Though hardly vital today, the lexical distinction persists.

The Sapir-Whorf hypothesis about culture-language correlations, to which so many Marxist linguists are indebted, itself demands careful scrutiny. Many of its factual claims are simply incorrect; furthermore, when carried to its logical conclusion it may well have some socially undesirable—perhaps even racist—consequences. Whorf himself was not a racist by any stretch of the imagination. His profound relativism, his glorification of linguistic and cultural diversity, are the very opposite of a belief in the intrinsic superiority of either Western languages or culture. Yet for all that, neither he nor his followers have approached Western and non-Western languages on an equal basis. If they did do so, if they looked for relationships between English or German language and culture in the same way as they have for Hopi and Shawnee, they might have been led to some self-evidently absurd conclusions. Consider, for example, the tense systems of the various European languages. English has an inflected present *(the baby cries)* and an inflected past *(the baby cried)*, but no inflected future. Rather, the future must be expressed by periphrasis *(the baby will cry)*. German, like English, has two inflected tenses (though their use is different), Spanish and French have five, and Russian has three. Given Whorf's claim about the interconnectedness of grammatical tense and time perception in Hopi, shouldn't one exist in Western languages as well? Why aren't the marked differences in the tense systems of English, German, Spanish, and Russian reflected in fundamentally different ways of viewing the passage of time and its compartmentalization?

Or take grammatical gender, which is found in most Indo-European languages. If the Hopi tense system conceals a metaphysics, then why doesn't the German gender system do so too? Why don't Germans "see" girls as neuters *(das Mädchen)* and battles as females *(die Schlacht)?* Or why doesn't the circumstance that the word for "sun" in German is feminine, and the word for "moon" masculine, but the reverse in French, reveal some fact about the difference between German and French culture and worldview?

To take another example, noted by the linguist Joseph Greenberg, employing the "same reasoning" as Whorf,

> a Frenchman who calls his kings Henri quatre *(Henry four)* and Louis treize *(Louis thirteen)* might draw the conclusion that English speakers who use the phrases "Henry the fourth" and "Louis the thirteenth" view each king of the same name as the same man appearing anew. He might even conjecture a belief in reincarnation of like-named kings. Further, a French observer might even be moved to conclusions similar to those entertained by Whorf for Hopi regarding the English conceptualization of time periods, by contrasting the French juillet quatorze *(July fourteen)* with English "July fourteenth."[5]

Needless to say, there is no evidence that the difference between English and French structure in this instance is reflected in a difference of worldview.

The determined quest for such correlations can lead to invidious distinctions between cultures and objectionable conclusions about national character. Part of the problem is the insuperable vagueness of the Sapir-Whorf hypothesis. Neither Sapir, Whorf, nor later advocates of the hypothesis have elucidated precisely which aspects of linguistic structure are the most likely to have broader repercussions on culture. Indeed, simply to characterize the components of a people's culture or worldview is difficult enough; to identify the specific features subject to linguistic influences seems an impossible and even potentially dangerous enterprise. Consider, for example, a widely read article on noun classes and folk taxonomy in Papago, an Indian language spoken in Arizona. The author notes that the number system in this language is strikingly different from English, in that it is relative rather than absolute. Unlike English, in which speakers can refer to "one tree," "two trees," etc., the Papago have a relativistic approach to number—their language forces them to specify whether there are more or fewer trees at some particular place than were expected, whether the trees are closer together or farther apart than is usual for that kind of tree, and so on. This fact, she concludes, has helped to determine that "Papago perception and behavior are along a sliding scale rather than in terms of a two-valued logic."[6] She goes on to demonstrate how Papago grammatical structure has left its mark on the everyday life of a speaker of the language: "Let me cite an anecdotal corroboration of this inference: I was told of a Papago who quit his job of sorting oranges because he found it impossible to make up his mind about good and bad oranges."[7]

The dangers implicit in such an account should be obvious. Even if there does exist some link between Papago grammar and the ability of the Papago to make certain types of discriminations—a possibility that cannot be ruled out *a priori*—there are other, far more obvious, reasons that could cause a Papago to have trouble holding down a job in agribusiness. Not to bring up any additional reasons that might prevent an Indian from succeeding at even a menial job in a dominant alien culture is irresponsible. And even worse, in the hands of an employer a conclusion like this one drawn from the Sapir-Whorf hypothesis could provide an easy excuse for the practice of racial discrimination in hiring. After all, what one's native language is is something completely beyond one's control. What would be the point of any program designed to improve the Papagos' employment opportunities if their language has locked them into a world in which the judgments they need to make on the job are impossible for them?

In short, while it is not unreasonable to believe that there might exist a Whorfian correlation between the grammar of a language and the worldview of the people speaking the language, there is to date little supporting evidence for such a correlation, and much reason to exert extreme caution in proposing one. And, we might add, much reason for Marxists to be cautious in concluding that Whorf's work supports the idea that the grammatical properties of a language are superstructural.

Still, it must be emphasized that to deny the superstructural nature of grammar is in no sense to deny the validity of a Marxist account of other aspects of language. Marxists have contributed to theories of language style, to discourse analysis, to an understanding of social norms governing language use, and much more. Indeed, even the many Marxist studies of how particular grammatical features have come to be correlated with social class (or sex, or occupational group, or whatever) have much to recommend them — as long as they do not insist that the correlation is a necessary one. If it were the case that Chomsky and other autonomous linguists advocated the reduction of language in all of its manifestations to autonomous rules, then indeed Marxist critics would have grounds for complaint. But, as we have seen, autonomous linguists do not do so. Chomsky has never made any claims at all about how the genuinely super-structural aspects of language should be analyzed. Linguistic competence for Chomsky encompasses only the ahistorical component of language.

Although Chomsky's notion of competence, his specific ideas concerning universal grammar, abstract deep structures, generative rules, and so on may well turn out to be deficient, there is nothing inherently un-Marxist about them. It is finally as senseless to speak of a Marxist theory of grammatical structure as a Marxist theory of genetic or atomic structure. And just as there are Marxist geneticists and atomic physicists, there are, as we have seen, Marxist generative grammarians as well. Joseph Emonds, for example, who investigates the structure of English subject pronouns and analyzes the social factors governing their use, is no more incongruous than a physicist who is committed to both the study of the structure of the atomic nucleus and the campaign against the proliferation of nuclear weapons.

This brings us to the question of whether autonomous linguistics and generative grammar in particular have any right to call themselves "scientific." It is hardly possible here to measure autonomous linguistics in its various forms against the many (conflicting) theories of what constitutes scientific methodology. Nevertheless, there is one universally recognized feature of science that distinguishes it from nonscientific pursuits, namely, its ability to lead to the *unexpected result:* the discovery that a set of principles arrived at through attention to one set of data has correctly predicted the behavior of phenomena not originally the subject of investigation. For example, Newton's laws of universal gravitation, based on his observations of the positions of celestial bodies, provided, for centuries to come, explanations of various terrestrial phenomena that Newton had not even considered when formulating his hypotheses.

The unexpected results of the autonomous orientation have been prodigious. Consider first an example from comparative linguistics. In 1878, Saussure (then twenty-one years old) was led to posit for Proto-Indo-European a series of sounds that had no direct descendents in any modern Indo-European language. Saussure's hypothesis that such sounds must have existed was based entirely on theoretical considerations. It was not until several decades later that the first extensive texts were discovered in Hittite, an ancient Indo-European language. Examination of these texts revealed that Hittite had sounds corresponding to those posited by Saussure in precisely the positions he had assigned to them in Proto-Indo-European. In other words, Saussure's hypothesis had been confirmed. The possibility that his discovery was a matter of "luck" or "coincidence" seems infinitesimally small. The inescapable conclusion is that the methodology of comparative linguistics is, in some pertinent sense, scientific.

The conceptions of synchronic autonomous linguistics have similarly been confirmed. Recent discoveries by researchers outside of linguistics proper provide independent corroboration for the autonomous linguistic view that the form of language exists independently of its content (i.e., competence independently of performance). For example, neurologists have found that the grammatical properties of language are represented in the brain separately from its functional properties, including semantic and pragmatic content. Under pathological conditions, form and function can even become dissociated from each other; many cases are documented in which, as a result of some cerebral trauma, a patient has maintained grammatical abilities yet has lost the ability to use language communicatively, or vice versa. Psychologists as well report cases of abnormal language acquisition, where form and function have become dissociated. There are now clinicians who specialize in treating children whose syntax is fluent but who cannot convey a coherent thought, and those whose communicative intent is obvious but cannot phrase that intent grammatically. Such discoveries give scientific credence to the hypothesis that grammatical form is autonomous.[8]

While autonomous linguists may have diffused the controversy somewhat and reassured many who feel threatened by their exclusionary stance by confining claims about the scientific status of their approach to a limited domain of inquiry, that confinement does relegate autonomy's function to a separate realm, apart from and unrelated to social concerns. In that sense, autonomy is vulnerable to the sociolinguists' moral critique. The basic presupposition of moral critique, that autonomous linguists disregard the role of the social factor when analyzing language, is indisputable. Rather, they investigate that aspect of language for which they believe the social factor to be irrelevant. Thus it goes without saying that anyone whose immediate concerns involve language in its social setting will not find the results of autonomous linguistics central to their interests. But it does not therefore follow that these results are completely irrelevant to the fulfillment of progressive political goals. For example, autonomy's assumptions have played a crucial role in the campaign to win general acceptance for the linguistic equality of all dialects—an idea which even the politically progressive segment of the general public resists. Anybody who now takes an introductory course in descriptive linguistics taught from any perspective learns that Black English and other nonstandard dialects are "real" languages, and that such dialectal phenomena as negative concord and the absence of number agreement are widespread among the world's languages. Generativists have added new force to egalitarianism, bringing to bear their technical understanding of generative rules to prove that a nonstandard construction is "linguistically normal."

Take a Black English sentence like *Didn't nobody see it,* which in that dialect is the simple negation of *Somebody saw it.* One might conclude from such a sentence that a fundamental difference exists between Black English and the standard dialect or, even, given the most uncharitable (i.e., racist) interpretation of Black English, that its speakers confuse the concepts of negating and questioning. But as William Labov has demonstrated, if one understands the operation of the relevant transformational rules in Standard English, one can see easily that the differences between it and Black English are completely trivial—the two dialects differ grammatically only in the most superficial way. Labov shows that *Didn't nobody see it*, rather than being a question form used as a declarative (which *would* be a radical difference from Standard English) is analogous to sentences of literary English like *Never did he see it* or *Nor did anybody see it*. He demonstrates that the Black English sentence is derived by a simple extension of the generative rule involved in the derivation of the latter two: the negative is placed at the beginning of the sentence along with the first verbal element. While the resultant sentence may manifest the same word order as a question, *Didn't nobody see it* is no more a question than is *Never did he see it.*[9]

Such careful, precise investigation is essential to adequately dispel a number of false ideas about the language of blacks, — in particular, the idea that it has a "primitive" grammatical system that constrains the ability of its speakers to think rationally. Indeed, the failure of black children in the schools has been blamed directly on the supposed grammatical inadequacies of Black English.[10] While it may be true that no racist will be daunted by the fact that the transformational rules of blacks are as complex and abstract as those of whites, the demonstration that the grammatical sophistication of black language is comparable to that of white language does undercut what might serve as a "scientific" basis for black inferiority.

Kenneth Hale, whose generativist work focuses on the indigenous languages of North America and Australia, also points to a progressive social implication of current theoretical research. He has suggested that in the native communities, the schools could make the grammatical analysis of the local language the center of the science curriculum. Through developing a "consciously experimental" attitude to their language, the students would learn the principles of scientific investigation and, with increasing awareness of the complexity and sophistication of their grammars, develop greater pride in their heritage.[11]

The principles of autonomous linguistics are also relevant to feminist concerns. In an early paper on the manifestation of sex roles in the speech differences between men and women, Robin Lakoff wrote that women literally have a *different language* from men, with differences at every linguistic level: phonological, syntactic, semantic, and pragmatic. If this were the case, then in order to succeed in a male-dominated world, a woman would literally have to become "bilingual." But the problems faced by bilingual speakers are well known: "Like many bilinguals, she may never really be master of either language, though her command of both is adequate enough for most purposes, she may never feel really comfortable using either, and never be certain that she is using the right one in the right place to the right person."[12]

Paradoxically, if Lakoff were correct, the barriers to women's equality would be all but insurmountable. By being forced not only to learn a second "language," but also having to master the intricacies involved in switching between the second and the first, a burden would be placed on women that, it would seem, would relegate them quite firmly to second-class status. Indeed, Lakoff comes close to claiming that "language" differences are a primary factor locking women into a subservient role in our culture.[13]

Virginia Valian has argued persuasively that Lakoff's pessimistic outlook is derived in large part from her failure to recognize the fundamental distinction of autonomous linguistics between language and speech (i.e., competence and performance). By conflating the two, Lakoff equates the necessity of mastering another stylistic level of *speech*, something that we all do many times in our lives without serious difficulty, with the arduous task of learning a second *language*. Valian writes:

> The *reductio ad absurdum* occurs because Lakoff confuses speech with language. An analogy with another field may clarify matters. Perhaps men and women add and multiply differently. That is not evidence for "women's mathematics" and "men's mathematics," but for different computational styles. The structure of mathematics is the same, no matter who uses it. Similarly, there is a difference between the English language and how people use that language, and nothing is served by obscuring that difference. . . .[14]

As the Lakoff-Valian exchange reveals, there are no easy definitions, no political labels that apply to these different approaches to language. Although one should not exaggerate the potential of autonomous linguistics for social influence, it is not, as many sociolinguists would have it, entirely without progressive social implications. By the same token, it is essential to stress that there is nothing inherently progressive about sociolinguistics.

North American sociolinguistic research, like North American social science in general, tends toward descriptive and statistical statements that rarely go beyond correlating some linguistic feature with some social factor. A typical research paper might, say, report on the conditions under which a Paraguayan villager will speak Guarani and the conditions under which he or she will speak Spanish. Such studies may be of general or specialized interest, but there is nothing intrinsically socially progressive about them. Presumably the information they reveal is of as much use to the ruling elite of the country as it is to its democratic opposition. Indeed, in most sociolinguistic studies potential relevance for good is offset by potential relevance for evil, particularly given the "value-free" rhetorical style that characterizes much work in this area.

A vivid illustration of the fact that sociolinguistics does not *ipso facto* aid the oppressed is provided by the Ford Foundation's granting patterns. The foundation has over the past few decades poured tens of millions of dollars into language and linguistics programs. Incredibly, the foundation gives *political* motivation for its refusal to fund generativist research: it objects to the fact that generativists "have isolated [the field] from the world of non-linguistic events and concentrated on abstract and formal theories about the nature and structure of language."[15] The Ford Foundation chooses to support those linguists who "have come to view the relevance of their discipline as most importantly defined by its ability to contribute to an understanding of society."[16] What sort of work has the Ford Foundation supported? Among other things, the research of the British sociologist Basil Bernstein, whose views have been described as "filtered through a strong bias against all forms of working-class behavior, so that middle class language is seen as superior in every respect,"[17] and a host of national language-planning projects carried out at the behest of less-than-liberal regimes such as those in Peru, Liberia, and the Philippines.

The point of all this is not to condemn academic sociolinguistics, but merely to stress once again that, as a social science, it will reflect all of the assumptions, prejudices, pressures, and conflicts that the social scientist faces in American society today. Sociolinguistic research, whatever its value, is no more intrinsically progressive than research in sociology, economics, history, or political science.

Are the conflicts in linguistics resolvable? Certainly the field is riddled with differences that appear irreconcilable. The view that language is degraded when treated as a system of structures and rules, that only triviality can emerge from the study of its role in society, or that the investigation of its poetic function is outside the domain of the field altogether reflect positions and priorities that go well beyond one's approach to language itself. And there are fundamental questions of empirical fact that are years, if not decades, from resolution. Does an understanding of linguistic structure provide a key to the structure of the human mind? Is there a causal connection between a people's worldview and the nature of its language? Is the social status of women reinforced by the differences in language between them and men? Such problems are difficult ones, to put it mildly, and the field is hardly likely to see harmony before more progress is made toward their solution.

But at the same time, it is crucial to stress that there is nothing essentially incompatible about the different *orientations* to language. The humanist can discuss language as an instrument of creativity and intellectual freedom without abutting on the question of its social role or its structure. Likewise, there is no principled incompatibility between the interests of the sociologically oriented linguist and those of the humanist and the grammarian. Why should the study of the social interfere with or detract from that of the aesthetic or the mental? And, since generative grammarians have been careful to confine their claims about autonomous structures and rules to a restricted subpart of language, their hypotheses should pose no threat to the interests or results of humanistically and sociologically oriented linguists. The goals of the three orientations are wholly complementary; the field of linguistics can, and should, accommodate each with its unique concerns and special contributions to the understanding of language.

NOTES

1. The Study of Language

1. The 1970s saw an apparent undermining of this traditional conception of language as a result of the degree of success achieved in teaching the sign language of the deaf to chimpanzees. However, as the results of these experiments became better understood, even some of the most enthusiastic proponents of the chimps-have-language hypothesis reevaluated their conclusions and returned to the idea of human linguistic uniqueness. See, for example, H. Terrace, *Nim* (New York: Alfred A. Knopf, 1979) and D. Premack, *The Mind of an Ape* (New York: Norton, 1983).

2. I. Robinson, *The New Grammarians' Funeral: A Critique of Noam Chomsky's Linguistics* (Cambridge: Cambridge University Press, 1975), p. 181.

3. W. La Barre, "What Linguists Tell Anthropologists," in *Report on the Ninth Annual Round Table Meeting on Linguistics and Language Studies*, ed. W. Austin (Washington, D.C.: Georgetown University Press, 1960), p. 74.

4. V. Fromkin and R. Rodman, *An Introduction to Language*, 3rd ed. (New York: Holt, Rinehart and Winston, 1983).

5. B. Croce, *Estetica Come Scienza dell'Espressione e Linguistica Generale* (Bari: Gius, Laterza, and Figli, 1902).

6. W. Labov, *The Study of Nonstandard English* (Champaign, Ill.: The National Council of Teachers of English, 1970), p. 183.

7. D. T. Langendoen, *Essentials of English Grammar* (New York: Holt, Rinehart and Winston, 1970), p. 3.

8. M. A. K. Halliday, "The Context of Linguistics," in *Georgetown University Round Table on Languages and Linguistics 1974*, ed. F. Dinneen (Washington, D.C.: Georgetown University Press, 1974), p. 178; G. Lakoff, Interview in *Discussing Language*, ed. Herman Parret (The Hague: Mouton, 1974), p. 178.

9. D. Hymes, "On Linguistic Theory, Communicative Competence, and the Education of Disadvantaged Children," in *Anthropological Perspectives on Education*," ed. M. Wax et al. (New York: Basic Books, 1971), p. 53.

10. For a particularly clear statement to this effect, see H. Haberland and J. Mey, "Editorial: Linguistics and Pragmatics," *Journal of Pragmatics* 1 (1977): 1–12.

11. J. P. Maher, "The Transformational-Generative Paradigm: A Silver Anniversary Polemic," *Forum Linguisticum* 5 (1980): 32; R. A. Hall, *Stormy Petrel Flies Again* (Watkins Glen, N.Y.: American Life Foundation, 1980), pp. 65–66.

12. N. Chomsky, *Language and Responsibility* (New York: Pantheon Books, 1979), p. 56.

13. Ibid., pp. 56–57.

2. The Rise of Autonomous Linguistics

1. W. Jones, "The Third Anniversary Discourse, on the Hindus" (1786). Reprinted in *A Reader in Nineteenth Century Historical Indo-European Linguistics*, ed. W. Lehmann (Austin:

University of Texas Press, 1967), p. 15. While Jones was not the first to suggest a relationship between Sanskrit and the European languages, previous suggestions to that effect seem not to have instigated a research program designed to make the relationship more precise.

2. J. Grimm, *Geschichte der deutschen Sprache*, vol. 1 (Leipzig: Weidmannsche Buchhandlung, 1848).

3. See J. R. Firth, *Papers in Linguistics, 1934–1951* (London: Oxford University Press, 1957), p. 161.

4. N. Chomsky, *Cartesian Linguistics* (New York: Harper and Row, 1966), p. 24.

5. Cited in G. Sampson, *Schools of Linguistics* (Stanford: Stanford University Press, 1980), p. 17.

6. A. F. Pott, *Etymologische Forschungen* . . . , vol. 1 (Lemgo: Meyersche Hof. Buchhandlung, 1833), p. xxvii.

7. H. S. Maine, *Village Communities in the East and West* (London: J. Murray, 1872), p. 51. For an interesting discussion on Maine's debt to contemporary linguistics, see J. Greenberg, "Linguistics as a Pilot Science," in *Themes in Linguistics: The 1970's*, ed. E. Hamp (The Hague: Mouton, 1973).

8. H. Paul, *Principles of the History of Language* (London: Longmans, Green, 1891).

9. F. de Saussure, *Course in General Linguistics* (New York: McGraw-Hill, 1966), p. 232.

3. Structural Linguistics

1. For representative statements from the leading structuralist schools on the autonomy of *langue*, see E. Sapir, *Selected Writings of Edward Sapir in Language, Culture, and Personality*, ed. D. Mandelbaum (Berkeley: University of California Press, 1949), p. 100; R. H. Robins, "General Linguistics in Great Britain 1930–1960," in *Trends in Modern Linguistics*, ed. C. Mohrmann et al. (Utrecht: Spectrum, 1963), p. 21; B. Trnka, "Linguistics and the Ideological Structure of the Period," in *The Linguistic School of Prague*, ed. J. Vachek (Bloomington: Indiana University Press, 1966), p. 158; A. Martinet, Interview in *Dis-*

cussing *Language,* ed. H. Parret (The Hague: Mouton, 1974), p. 244; H. Spang-Hanssen, "Glossematics," in *Trends in European and American Linguistics 1930–1960,* ed. C. Mohrmann et al. (Utrecht: Spectrum, 1961), p. 130.

2. F. de Saussure, *Course in General Linguistics* (New York: McGraw-Hill, 1966), p. 111.

3. A. L. Kroeber, "Culture," in *Papers of the Peabody Museum in American Archaeology and Ethnology,* ed. A. L. Kroeber and C. H. Kluckhohn (Cambridge: Harvard University Press, 1952), p. 124.

4. C. Kluckhohn, "Common Humanity and Diverse Cultures," in *The Human Meaning of the Social Sciences* (New York: Meridian Books, 1959), p. 262.

5. See K. Pike, *Language in Relation to a Unified Theory of the Structure of Human Behavior* (Glendale, Calif.: Summer Institute of Linguistics, 1954); H. Lasswell et al., *Language of Politics: Studies in Quantitative Semantics* (New York: George W. Stewart, 1949); H. Whitehall, "From Linguistics to Criticism," *Kenyon Review* 13 (1951): 710–14.

6. C. Lévi-Strauss, "Remarks," in *An Appraisal of Anthropology Today,* ed. S. Tax et al. (Chicago: University of Chicago Press, 1953), pp. 350–51.

7. A. Schaff, *Structuralism and Marxism* (Oxford: Pergamon Press, 1978), p. 24.

8. For more detailed discussion of the development of American structural linguistics, see D. Hymes and J. Fought, *American Structuralism* (The Hague: Mouton, 1981).

9. E. Sapir, *Language* (New York: Harcourt, Brace, and World, 1921), p. 219.

10. V. Fromkin and R. Rodman, *An Introduction to Language,* 3rd ed. (New York: Holt, Rinehart and Winston, 1983), p. 12.

11. L. Bloomfield, "Why a Linguistic Society?" *Language* 1 (1925): 2.

12. J. Gonda, "The Comparative Method as Applied to Indonesian Languages," *Lingua* 1 (1948): 86–101; G. Trager, review of *Lingua,* vol. 1, *IJAL* 14 (1948): 209.

13. B. Malmberg, *New Trends in Linguistics: An Orientation*

(Lund: Institute of Phonetics, University of Lund, 1964), pp. 183–84.

14. E. Sturtevant, "Report of the Special Committee of the Linguistic Institute," *Bulletin of the Linguistic Society of America* 13 (1940): 83.

15. S. Newman, review of B. Davis and R. O'Cain, *First Person Singular*, in *Historiographia Linguistica* 9 (1982): 139.

16. D. Hymes and J. Fought, *American Structuralism*, p. 46.

17. American Council of Learned Societies, *Report of the Commission on the Humanities* (1964), pp. 152–58.

18. J. Barzun, *The House of Intellect* (New York: Harper and Row, 1959), p. 243.

19. G. Nunberg, "The Decline of Grammar" (prepublication version of a paper that appeared in *Atlantic*, December 1983), pp. 15–16.

20. Ibid., p. 20.

21. J. Simon, *Paradigms Lost* (New York: Clarkson Potter, 1980), p. x.

22. Ibid., p. 41.

23. Ibid., p. 148.

24. R. Hall, *Linguistics and Your Language* (Garden City, N.Y.: Anchor Books, 1960), p. 29.

25. H. Whitehall, "From Linguistics to Criticism," p. v.

26. L. Bloomfield, *Linguistic Aspects of Science* (Chicago: University of Chicago Press, 1939).

27. R. Jakobson, "The Twentieth Century in European and American Linguistics: Movements and Continuity," in *The European Background of American Linguistics*, ed. H. Hoenigswald (Dordrecht: Foris, 1979), p. 170.

28. R. Hall, "The State of Linguistics: Crisis or Reaction?" *Italica* 23 (1946): 33–34.

29. L. Spitzer, "The State of Linguistics: Crisis or Reaction?" *Modern Language Notes* 71 (1946): 499.

30. R. Hall, "Some Recent Developments in American Linguistics," *Neuphilologische Mitteilungen* 70 (1969): 15.

31. C. Hockett, review of A. Martinet, *Phonology as Functional Phonetics*, in *Language* 27 (1951): 333–42; A. Martinet,

"Structural Linguistics," in *Anthropology Today: An Encyclopedic Inventory*, ed. A. L. Kroeber (Chicago: University of Chicago Press, 1953), pp. 574–86.

32. D. Hymes and J. Fought, *American Structuralism*, p. 119.

33. J M. Cowan, "Linguistics at War," in *The Uses of Anthropology*, ed. W. Goldschmidt (special publication of the American Anthropological Association, no. 11, Washington, D.C., 1979), p. 159.

34. D. Hymes and J. Fought, *American Structuralism*, p. 16.

35. W. Parker, *The National Interest and Foreign Languages* (Washington, D.C.: U.S. Government Printing Office, 1954), p. 123.

36. For discussion, see L. Bloomfield, "Twenty-one Years of the Linguistic Society," *Language* 22 (1946): 1–3.

37. M. Graves and J M. Cowan, "Excerpt of *Report of the First Year's Operation of the Intensive Language Program of the American Council of Learned Societies*," *Hispania* 25 (1942): 490.

38. M. Joos, *Readings in Linguistics* (Washington, D.C.: American Council of Learned Societies, 1957), p. 108.

39. R. Hall, "American Linguistics, 1925–1950," *Archivum Linguisticum* 3 (1951): 106.

40. *FSI Catalog* (Washington, D.C., 1949), p. 2.

41. Ibid., p. 7.

42. J. B. Carroll, *The Study of Language* (Cambridge: Harvard University Press, 1951), p. 182.

43. M. Graves, *A Neglected Facet of the National Security Problem* (Washington, D.C., 1950), p. 1.

44. M. Graves, comments in the session entitled "Meeting the Government's Need in Languages," in *Report on the Second Annual Round Table Meeting on Linguistics and Language Teaching*, ed. J. De Francis (Washington, D.C.: Georgetown University Press, 1951), p. 1.

45. A. Marckwardt, "Linguistics and the NDEA," *Language Learning* 9 (1959): iv.

46. K. Mildenberger, "The National Defense Education Act and Linguistics," in *Report of the Eleventh Annual Round Table Meeting on Linguistics and Language Studies*, ed. B. Choseed

(Washington, D.C.: Georgetown University Press, 1962), p. 161.

47. J. Hewitt, remarks at the opening ceremony of the School of Oriental Studies, *Bulletin of the School of Oriental Studies* 1 (1917): 26.

48. For general discussion, see R. H. Robins, "General Linguistics."

49. E. Pike, "Historical Sketch," in *The Summer Institute of Linguistics*, ed. R. Brend and K. Pike (The Hague: Mouton, 1977), p. 11.

50. C. F. Voegelin, cited in E. Wallis and M. Bennett, *Two Thousand Tongues To Go* (New York: Harper and Row), p. 131.

51. A voluminous literature exists on the political and cultural consequences of SIL work. For representative critiques, see S. Hvalkof and P. Aaby, eds., *Is God an American?* (Copenhagen: International Work Group for Indigenous Affairs, 1981); D. Stoll, *Fishers of Men or Founders of Empire?* (London: Zed Press, 1982); "The Wycliffe Bible Translators: Not Telling the Whole Story," *The Other Side*, February 1983, pp. 5–7. For a defense of SIL, see R. L. Canfield, "Accusation as 'Anthropology,'" *Reviews in Anthropology* 10 (1983): 55–61; W. Christie, review of *Is God an American?* in *Languages for Peace*, October 1983; W. Kornfield, "'Fishers of Men or Founders of Empire?,'" *Evangelical Missions Quarterly*, October 1983, pp. 308–13; J. Yost, "We Have a Mandate," *The Other Side*, February 1983, pp. 7–9.

4. The Chomskyan Revolution

1. H. Maclay, "Linguistics: Overview," in *Semantics*, ed. D. Steinberg and L. Jakobovits (Cambridge: Cambridge University Press, 1971), p. 163; J. Lyons, *Noam Chomsky* (New York: Viking Press, 1970), p. 1; R. H. Robins, "Malinowski, Firth, and Context of Situation," in *Social Anthropology and Language*, ed. E. Ardener (London: Tavistock, 1971), p. 33.

2. See J. Katz and P. Postal, *An Integrated Theory of Linguistic Descriptions* (Cambridge: MIT Press, 1964); N. Chomsky, *Aspects of the Theory of Syntax* (Cambridge: MIT Press, 1965).

3. See N. Chomsky and M. Halle, *The Sound Pattern of English* (New York: Harper and Row, 1968).

4. See J. R. Ross, *Constraints on Variables in Syntax* (Unpublished MIT dissertation, 1968).

5. See, for example, M. Lane, *Introduction to Structuralism* (New York: Basic Books, 1970), pp. 28–29; R. De George and F. De George, *The Structuralists* (Garden City, N.Y.: Doubleday, 1972), p. xx.

6. N. Chomsky, review of B. F. Skinner, *Verbal Behavior*, in *Language* 35 (1959): 26–57.

7. For development of this point, see H. Bracken, "Essence, Accident, and Race," *Hermathena* 116 (1974): 81–96.

8. N. Chomsky, *American Power and the New Mandarins* (New York: Vintage Books, 1969), p. 9. On the issue of Vietnam, see also *At War With Asia* (New York: Pantheon Books, 1970) and *For Reasons of State* (New York: Pantheon Books, 1973).

9. See Chomsky, *American Power; Towards a New Cold War* (New York: Pantheon Books, 1982); N. Chomsky and E. S. Herman, *The Political Economy of Human Rights* (Montreal: Black Rose Books, 1979).

10. For the most fully developed exposition of Chomsky's anarchosyndicalism, see his *Radical Priorities* (Montreal: Black Rose Books, 1981).

11. N. Chomsky, *Language and Responsibility* (New York: Pantheon Books, 1979), p. 3.

12. N. Chomsky, "Linguistics and Politics," *New Left Review* 57 (1969): 31.

13. J. Thorne, Review of P. Postal, *Constituent Structure*, in *Journal of Linguistics* 1 (1965): 74.

14. For discussion and a historical overview, see C. Hempel, "Empiricist Criteria of Cognitive Significance: Problems and Changes," in *Aspects of Scientific Explanation*, ed. C. Hempel (New York: Free Press, 1965).

15. See K. Lashley, "The Problem of Serial Order in Behavior," in *Cerebral Mechanisms in Behavior*, ed. L. A. Jeffers (New

York: Wiley, 1951); C. W. Mills, *The Sociological Imagination* (New York: Oxford University Press, 1959).

16. G. Lakoff, interview in *Discussing Language*, ed. Herman Parret (The Hague: Mouton, 1974), p. 170.

17. W. Chafe, *Meaning and the Structure of Language* (Chicago: University of Chicago Press, 1970), p. 2.

18. For this line of argumentation, see S. Murray, "Gatekeepers and the 'Chomskyan Revolution,'" *Journal of the History of the Behavioral Sciences* 16 (1980): 73–88. For a reply to Murray, see F. Newmeyer, "Has There Been a 'Chomskyan Revolution' in Linguistics?" *Language* 62 (1986): 1–18.

19. J. Searle, "Chomsky's Revolution in Linguistics," *New York Review of Books*, June 29, 1972, p. 17.

20. See R. Hall, "Fact and Fiction in Grammatical Analysis," *Foundations of Language* 1 (1965): 337–45; G. Herdan, "Götzendämmerung at M.I.T.," *Zeitschrift für Phonetik* 21 (1968): 223–31; J. P. Maher, "The Transformational-Generative Paradigm: A Silver Anniversary Polemic," *Forum Linguisticum* 5 (1980): 1–35.

21. Personal communication, March 1, 1971.

22. Citation of Chomsky's acknowledgments was common practice in Soviet critiques for a time. See also J. S. Thompson, "The Reactionary Idealistic Foundations of Noam Chomsky's Linguistics," *Literature and Ideology* 4 (1969): 1–20.

23. N. Chomsky, "Human Nature: Justice Versus Power," in *Reflexive Water: The Basic Concerns of Mankind*, ed. F. Elders (London: Souvenir Press, 1974), p. 195.

24. For extensive discussion of generative semantics, see F. Newmeyer, *Linguistic Theory in America* (New York: Academic Press, 1986).

25. R. Lakoff, "Language and Woman's Place," *Language in Society* 2 (1973): 45–79.

26. G. Lakoff, interview, p. 172.

27. Ibid., p. 153.

28. R. Lakoff, "Pluralism in Linguistics," *Berkeley Studies in Syntax and Semantics* 1 (1974): xiv–23.

29. For an introduction to Piaget's views on language, see his book *The Language and Thought of the Child* (Cleveland: Meridian Books, 1955). *Language and Learning*, ed. M. Piatelli-Pal-

marini (Cambridge: Harvard University Press, 1980) is devoted to a major debate between Chomsky and Piaget.

30. See N. Chomsky, *Lectures on Government and Binding* (Dordrecht: Foris, 1981).

31. Most recently in a 1982 survey undertaken by the National Research Council.

32. J. P. Maher, "The Transformational-Generative Paradigm," p. 6.

33. N. Chomsky, *The Generative Enterprise* (Dordrecht: Foris, 1982), p. 8 (emphasis added).

34. Ibid., pp. 42–43.

5. The Opposition to Autonomous Linguistics

1. P. Goodman, *Speaking and Language: Defense of Poetry* (New York: Vintage Books, 1972).

2. G. Steiner, *After Babel: Aspects of Language and Translation* (Oxford: Oxford University Press, 1975), p. 108.

3. R. Harris, *The Language Makers* (Ithaca: Cornell University Press, 1980).

4. I. Robinson, *The New Grammarians' Funeral: A Critique of Noam Chomsky's Linguistics* (Cambridge: Cambridge University Press, 1975), pp. 102–3.

5. Ibid., p. 48.

6. For two examples, see D. T. Langendoen, "The Problem of Linguistic Theory in Relation to Language Behavior: A Tribute to Paul Goodman," *Daedalus* 102 (1973): 195–201; S. J. Keyser, review of G. Steiner, *After Babel*, in *New Review* 2 (1975): 63–66.

7. K. Marx and F. Engels, *The German Ideology* (New York: International Publishers, 1970), pp. 50–51.

8. V. N. Vološinov, *Marxism and the Philosophy of Language* (New York: Seminar Press, 1973). Many now believe, however, that this book was actually authored by Vološinov's teacher, the literary critic M. M. Bakhtin.

9. J. Emonds, "Grammatically Deviant Prestige Dialect Constructions," in *A Festschift for Sol Saporta*, ed. by M. Brame, H. Contreras, and F. Newmeyer (Seattle: Noit Amrofer, 1985).

10. Vološinov, p. 66.

11. Ibid., p. 71.

12. Ibid., p. 19.

13. Ibid., p. 19.

14. E. Sapir, abstract of a paper entitled "Conceptual Categories in Primitive Languages," presented to the National Academy of Sciences, *Science* 74 (1931): 578.

15. B. L. Whorf, *Language, Thought, and Reality: Selected Writings of Benjamin Lee Whorf,* ed. J. B. Carroll (Cambridge: MIT Press, 1956), p. 57.

16. Ibid., pp. 57–58.

17. Ibid., p. 58.

18. See for example, F. Rossi-Landi, *Ideologies of Linguistic Relativity* (The Hague: Mouton, 1973).

19. M. K. Adler, *Marxist Linguistic Theory and Communist Practice* (Hamburg: Helmut Buske Verlag, 1980), pp. 56–57.

20. R. Williams, *Marxism and Literature* (Oxford: Oxford University Press, 1977), p. 27.

21. Ibid., p. 28.

22. D. Silverman and B. Torode, *The Material Word: Some Theories of Language and its Limits* (London: Routledge and Kegan Paul, 1980), p. 43.

23. For the most thorough discussion of Marr's views, see L. Thomas, *The Linguistic Theories of N. Ja. Marr* (Berkeley: University of California Press, 1957).

24. See H. Rubenstein, "The Recent Conflict in Soviet Linguistics," *Language* 27 (1951): 281–87.

25. Ibid., pp. 284–85.

26. The contributions have been translated and published as *The Soviet Linguistic Controversy,* ed. J. V. Murra, R. M. Hankin, and F. Holling (New York: King's Crown Press, 1951). Stalin's contributions appear separately in *Marxism and Linguistics* (New York: International Publishers, 1951).

27. Murra et al., p. 76.

28. Ibid., p. 81.

29. Ibid., p. 91.

30. Stalin, *Marxism and Linguistics,* pp. 23–24.

31. Ibid., pp. 9–10.

32. Western journalists from the start raised the possibility that nationalism lay behind Stalin's actions, a charge rebutted in M. Schlauch's appendix to Stalin's *Marxism and Linguistics*.

33. The Engels quote is from Murra et al., p. 60, who cite "K. Marx and F. Engels, *Letters*, 4th edition, pp. 375–6." The two other references may be found in F. Engels, *Dialectics of Nature* (New York: International Publishers, 1940 [1882]), pp. 282–84 and K. Marx, "Introduction to a Critique of Political Economy," supplementary text to K. Marx and F. Engels, *The German Ideology* (London: Lawrence and Wishart, 1970), p. 126.

34. D. Hymes, *Foundations in Sociolinguistics* (Philadelphia: University of Pennsylvania Press, 1974), p. 203.

35. D. Hymes, "Sociolinguistics and the Ethnography of Speaking," in *Social Anthropology and Language*, ed. E. Ardener (London: Tavistock, 1971), p. 49.

36. D. Hymes, "Introduction: Traditions and Paradigms," in *Studies in the History of Linguistics: Traditions and Paradigms*, ed. D. Hymes (Bloomington: Indiana University Press, 1974), p. 22.

37. H. Haberland and J. Mey, "Editorial: Linguistics and Pragmatics," *Journal of Pragmatics* 1 (1977): 4.

38. E. Kuykendall, "Feminist Linguistics in Philosophy," in *Sexist Language: A Modern Philosophical Analysis*, ed. M. Vetterling-Braggin (Totowa, N.J.: Littlefield, Adams, 1981), p. 132.

39. B. Williams, review of N. Chomsky, *Reflections on Language*, in *New York Review of Books*, November 11, 1976, p. 44.

6. Some Thoughts on the Autonomy Controversy

1. N. Chomsky, *Language and Mind* (New York: Harcourt Brace Jovanovich, 1972), p. 1.

2. N. Chomsky, *Aspects of the Theory of Syntax* (Cambridge: MIT Press, 1965), p. 4.

3. Ibid., p. 15.

4. D. Hymes, "Competence and Performance in Linguistic Theory," in *Language Acquisition: Models and Methods*, ed. R. Huxley and E. Ingram (New York: Academic Press, 1971), pp. 10–11.

5. J. Greenberg, "Concerning Inferences from Linguistic to Nonlinguistic Data," in *Language in Culture,* ed. H. Hoijer (Chicago: University of Chicago Press, 1954), p. 14.

6. M. Mathiot, "Noun Classes and Folk Taxonomy in Papago," in *Language in Culture and Society,* ed. D. Hymes (New York: Harper and Row, 1964), p. 160.

7. Ibid.

8. For a survey of the neurological and psychological evidence supporting autonomy, see F. Newmeyer, *Grammatical Theory: Its Limits and Its Possibilities* (Chicago: University of Chicago Press, 1983).

9. W. Labov, *The Study of Nonstandard English* (Champaign, Ill.: National Council of Teachers of English, 1970), p. 40.

10. See, for example, the papers in *Pre-School Education Today,* ed. F. M. Hechinger (New York: Doubleday, 1966). For rebuttal, see W. Labov, op. cit.

11. See K. Hale, "Linguistics and Local Languages in a Science Curriculum for Bilingual/Bicultural Programs" (Unpublished paper, MIT, 1980).

12. R. Lakoff, "Language and Women's Place," *Language in Society* 2 (1973): 48.

13. Lakoff writes: "The ultimate effect of these discrepancies is that women are systematically denied access to power, on the grounds that they are not capable of holding it as demonstrated by their linguistic behavior along with other aspects of their behavior," p. 48.

14. V. Valian, "Linguistics and Feminism," in *Sexist Language: A Modern Philosophical Analysis,* ed. M. Vetterling-Braggin (Totowa, N.J.: Littlefield, Adams, 1981), p. 72.

15. M. Fox with B. Skolnick, *Language in Education: Problems and Prospects in Research and Teaching* (New York: The Ford Foundation, 1975), p. 6.

16. Ibid.

17. W. Labov, "The Logic of Nonstandard English," in *Georgetown University Round Table on Languages and Linguistics 1969* (Washington: Georgetown University Press, 1970), p. 4.

INDEX

Page numbers in italics refer to quotations.

Black English, 45, 112, 123, 135–36, 144–45, 163n. 10
Bloch, Bernard: *Outline of Linguistic Analysis*, 53
Bloomfield, Leonard, *41*, 47, 48, 52, 154n. 11, 155n. 26, 156n. 36; *Outline Guide for the Practical Study of Foreign Languages*, 53
Boas, Franz, 40, 52; *The Handbook of American Indian Languages*, 40
Bopp, Franz, *23*

Carroll, John B., 54, 156n. 42
Celtic languages, 18
Chomsky, Noam, vii, 7, *12–13*, 62, 65–97, 152nn. 12–13, 158nn. 2–3, 6, 160nn. 33–34; *Aspects of the Theory of Syntax*, 74, *86*; on creativity, *79–80*; criticism of, 12–13, 76, 77, 86–87, 91, 95, 103–4, 113, 121–23, 159n. 22, 162n. 39; Government-Binding Theory, 93, 160n. 30; international following, 93; on linguistic theory, 66–73, *130*, 141, 162nn. 1–3; political views, 73, 76, *77–80*, 87, 121, 158nn. 8–12, 159n. 23; and structuralism, 72–73; *Syntactic Structures*, 65–66, 73–74
Christianity: and linguistics, 59–61
Class distinctions in language. *See* Prescriptive grammar; Sociological linguistics
Classical philology, 22, 102
Cognition, 7, *73*, 75. *See also* Language: as human attribute
Cognitive psychology. *See* Psycholinguistics
Communication: animal, 75; human, 3, 5. *See also* Sociological linguistics
Comparative jurisprudence, 25–26

Comparative linguistics, 17–28, 118–19, 137, 142
Competence and performance. *See* Langue-parole dichotomy
Computer technology and linguistic research, 4, 93–94, 120
Conservatism. *See* Prescriptive grammar
Coordinate Structure Constraint, 70, 74–75
Cowan, J. Milton, 52, 53, 156nn. 33, 37
Croce, Benedetto, 10, 152n. 5

Darwin, Charles R., 6, 25
Depersonalization of language, 102–3
Derrida, Jacques, 104 n
Diachrony, 26, 31
Discourse analysis. *See* Sociological linguistics
Double negatives. *See* Negative concord

Egalitarianism in linguistics, 39–44, 143–44, 145; public resistance to 43, 46. *See also* Linguistic scholarship: conflict in
Emonds, Joseph, 108, 141, 160n. 9
Empiricism. *See* Methodology of linguistics, empiricist
Engels, Friedrich, 6, 25, *105–6*, *119*, 160n. 7, 162n. 32
English language, 19, 33, 43, 67, 70–71, 134, 135, 144–45
Equality of languages. *See* Egalitarianism in linguistics
Esperanto, 107
Evolution, Darwinian model of, 24–25

Feminism in linguistic research, 89, 90, 122, 124, 146–47, 162n. 38
Financial support for linguistic re-

search. *See* Linguistic scholarship, government sponsorship of

Folk taxonomy, 139–40, 163nn. 6–7

Ford Foundation: grants for linguistic research, 148–49, 163nn. 15–16

Foreign Service Institute (FSI), 54

Formalist movement, 35, 90

Foucault, Michael, 36

Fought, John, vii, *42–43*, *51*, 52, 154n. 8, 155n. 16, 156nn. 32, 34

Fromkin, V., 9, *40–41*, 152n. 4, 154n. 10

FSI. *See* Foreign Service Institute

Funding of linguistic research. *See* Linguistic scholarship, government sponsorship of; Ford Foundation

Gaines, Edmund P., *85–86*, 94

Gender (grammatical), 138

Generative semantics, 88–89, 90–91, 92, 93, 159n. 24

Germanic languages, 19, 20

God, 114

Gonda, J., 41, 154n. 12

Goodman, Paul: *Speaking and Language: Defense of Poetry*, 103, 160n. 1

Gothic languages, 18

Government and linguistic research. *See* Linguistic scholarship, government sponsorship of

Grammar, 6, 8–9, 10, 27, 33–34, 40–41, 134–36, 137, 138; generative or transformational, 67–75, 80–81, 88–89, 92–95, 132–33

Graves, Mortimer, 51, 52, 54–*55*, *56*, 156nn. 37, 43–44

Greek language, 5, 18, 19

Greenberg, Joseph, 138, 163n. 5

Grimm, Jacob, 19, *20*, 22 n, 153n. 2

Haberland, Hartmut, *122*, 152n. 10, 162n. 37

Hale, Kenneth, vii, 145–46, 163n. 11

Hall, Robert A., 43, *44*, *49–50*, *53–54*, 152n. 11, 155nn. 28, 30, 156n. 39, 159n. 20; *Leave Your Language Alone!*, 43, 155n. 24

Halle, Morris, vii, 68, 71, 84, 158n. 3

Halliday, M. A. K., *11*, 152n. 8

Harris, Roy, *The Language Makers*, 103, 160n. 3

Harris, Zellig, 42

Hewitt, John, *57–58*, 157n. 47

Historical linguistics, 9

History of linguistics, 17–28, 142

Hittite language, 142

Hockett, Charles, 50, 155n. 31

Hopi language, 110–11, 137, 138

Human interaction. *See* Communication, human

Human linguistic ability. *See* Language, as human attribute

Humanistic linguistics, 4–5, 8–9, 10, 13–14, 48, 58, 102–4, 130, 132

Humboldt, Wilhelm von, 22 n

Hymes, Dell, *11*, *42–43*, *51*, 52, *121–22*, 130–*31*, 152n. 9, 154n. 8, 155n. 16, 156nn. 32, 34, 162nn. 34–36, n. 4

Ideology and linguistics, 40, 134, 139–40, 161n. 18

ILP. *See* Intensive Language Program

Indigenous and colonial languages. *See* Third World nations, languages of

Indo-European languages, hypothesis of, 18–19, 142, 152–53n. 1

Indonesian languages, 41

Industry and linguistic research, 94, 125 n. *See also* Linguistic

Industry and linguistic research (*continued*)
   scholarship, government sponsorship of
Innate language capacity, 74, 76, 91
Intensive Language Program (ILP), 52
Interdisciplinary approach to linguistics, 49
Internal principle of life. *See* Biology and lingustics
International Congress of Linguistics, 82
International language, 107

Jacobson, Roman, 10, 35, 36, 37, 155n. 27
Jones, William, Sir, *17–18*, 22 n, 152–53n. 1
Joos, Martin, 53, 156n. 38

Kawi language of Java, 22 n
Kluckhohn, Clyde, 36, 154n. 4
Kroeber, A. L., 35–*36*, 154n. 3, 156n. 31

La Barre, W., *7*, 152n. 3
Labov, William, vii, 10, 144–45, *149*, 152n. 5, 163nn. 9, 17
Lacan, Jacques, 36, 104 n
Lakoff, George, *11*, *81–82*, *89*, 90, 152n. 8, 159nn. 16, 26–27
Lakoff, Robin, 89, *90*, *146–47*, 159nn. 25, 28, 163nn. 12–13
Langendoen, D. T., *11*, 152n. 7, 160n. 6
Language: acquisition of, 73, 74–75, 76, 91, 143 (*see also* Psycholinguistics); analysis of, 4; and computer programming, 4; as human attribute, 3, 6, 75–76, 79, 151n. 1; pervasiveness of, 3–4; physical embodiment of, 8; as a social product, 106; teaching of, 8, 45, 50,

51–52, 53, 54, 145–46
Language (journal), 95
Language-class linkages. *See* Sociological linguistics
Language in Society (journal), 124
Language instruction. *See* Language: teaching of
Langue-parole dichotomy, 32, 33, 34, 35, 72, 103, 113, 147, 153–54n. 1
Lees, Robert B., 81
Lévi-Strauss, Claude, 36, 41 n, 154n. 6
Linguistic changes and the unconscious, 6–7
Linguistic Inquiry (journal), 95
Linguistic scholarship, 9, 10, 35, 36, 37, 41–62; academic environment, 46–47, 50–51, 80–81, 83, 90, 93, 96, 104 n, 118–19; church support of 59–61; competing orientations in, 10–11, 13, 48–50, 80–81, 101–5, 108, 111, 118–19, 149–50; conflict in, 41–43, 44–45, 50, 118–19; government sponsorship of, in Great Britain, 57–59; government sponsorship of, in the United States, 51–57, 84–88, 124–25; political orientation in, 22 n, 37, 44–45, 50, 52, 60–61, 81–82, 89, 118; purpose of, 10–11, 149–50. *See also* Structuralism
Linguistic Society of America, 41, 42, 43, 53, 95
Linguistic value of dialects. *See* Egalitarianism in linguistics
Literary output of a language. *See* Egalitarianism in linguistics
Literature and linguistics, 9–10, 36, 104, 120
Lithuanian language, 19
LSA. *See* Linguistic Society of America

Lukoff, Fred, 71
Lyell, Charles, 6, 25
Lyons, John, *65*, 157n. 1

Machine translation, 85–86, 87–88, 119
Maclay, Howard, *65*, 157n. 1
Maine, Henry, Sir, 25–*26*, 153n. 7
Malmberg, Bertil, 42, 154n. 13
Mansfield Amendment to an appropriations bill, 87
Marckwardt, Albert, *56–57*, 156n. 45
Marr, Nikolaj Jakovlevič, 115–17, 118, 119, 161n. 23
Martinet, André, 38, 50–51, 153n. 1, 155–56n. 31
Marx, Karl, 6, 25, *105–6*, 160n. 7
Marxist views in linguistics, 11, 36, 38, 105–9, 111, 112–13, 114–15, 133, 140–41
Massachusetts Institue of Technology (MIT), 84–85, 87, 95
Meaning. *See* Semantics
Melčuk, I. A., 120
Methodology of linguistics, 21, 39, 47, 141–42; empiricist, 47–48, 49, 77, 80–81, 158nn. 14, 15. *See also* Chomsky, Noam
Mey, Jacob, *122*, 152n. 10, 162n. 37
Mildenberger, Kenneth W., *57*, 156n. 46
Mind, 75
Moral issues in linguistics, 120–21, 122
Morphology. *See* Grammar

National Defense Education Act, 56–57
Nationalism in linguistics, 118, 162n. 32
Natural sciences approach to languages. *See* Autonomous linguistics
NDEA. *See* National Defense Education Act

Negative concord, 134–35, 144–45
Neurolinguistics, 125, 143, 163n. 8. *See also* Language: physical embodiment of
Nonliterary languages. *See* Egalitarianism in linguistics
Nonstandard varieties of English. *See* Egalitarianism in linguistics
Nunberg, Geoffrey, vii, *44–45*, 155nn. 19–20

Papago language, 139–40, 163nn. 6–7
Pedagogical applications of linguistics. *See* Language: teaching of
Permissiveness in language. *See* Egalitarianism in linguistics
Pervasiveness of language. *See* Language, pervasiveness of
Phenomenology, 38
Philosophy and linguistics, 5,7, 47, 73
Phonetics, 8–9
Phonology, 9, 33, 68, 71
Piaget, Jean, 91, 159n. 29
Pidgin and creole languages, 124
Pike, Eunice V., *60*, 157n. 49
Poetics, 4–5, 8, 102–4, 131–32
Possible human language. *See* Chomsky, Noam, on linguistic theory
Postal, Paul, 81, 158n. 13
Pott, August F., *23*, 153n. 6
Pragmatics. *See* Sociological linguistics
Prague School, 35, 37
Prescriptive grammar, 44–45, 46
Primitive languages. *See* Egalitarianism in linguistics
Profession of linguistics. *See* Linguistic scholarship
Protolanguage, 18–19, 142
Psychoanalysis, 36
Psycholinguistics, 9, 73, 91, 92, 125, 132

Psychology and linguistics, 6–7, 47, 73

Race distinctions and the language. *See* Prescriptive grammar
Rationalism, 7, 74, 77
Regulation of language. *See* Prescriptive grammar
Research Laboratory of Electronics at the Massachusetts Institute of Technology (RLE), 84–85
Robins, R. H., vii, *65*, 153n. 1, 157n. 1
Robinson, Ian, *4*, *103–4*, 151n. 2, 160nn. 4–5
Rodman, R., *9*, *40–41*, 152n. 4, 154n. 10
Romance Philology (journal), 53–54
Romantic movement, 19–20

Sanskrit language, 17–18, 19
Sapir, Edward, 10, *40*, 41, 48, 52, *110*, 153n. 1, 154n. 9, 161n. 14
Sapir-Whorf hypothesis, 110–11, 137, 139, 140
Saporta, Sol, 83
Šaumjan, S. K., 120
Saussure, Ferdinand de, *27–28*, 31, 36, 104 n, 109, 142, 153n. 9, 154n. 2; *Cours de Linguistique Générale*, 31–34
Schaff, Adam, 38, 154n. 7
Schleicher, August, 23–24
School of Oriental and African Studies (SOAS), 57–59
Schuchardt, Hugo, 124
Scientific linguistics. *See* Methodology of linguistics
Searle, John, *83*, 159n. 19
Semantics, 9, 48–49, 68
Sentence structure. *See* Chomsky, Noam, on linguistic theory
SIL. *See* Summer Institute of Linguistics

Silverman, David: *The Material Word, 114*, 161n. 22
Simon, John, *45*, 155nn. 21–23
Skinner, B. F., 73, 158n. 6
SOAS. *See* School of Oriental and African Studies
Social exchange. *See* Sociological linguistics
Social nature of language. *See* Sociological linguistics
Sociological linguistics, 5, 7, 8, 10, 13–14, 58, 72, 92–93, 104–26, 130, 131, 133, 138–41, 143–44, 145, 146, 147–50
Soviet linguistics, 114–20
Speech, 32; as human attribute, 3; perception and production of, 9; social acceptability of, 46
Spencer, Herbert, 25
Spitzer, Leo, 50, 155n. 29
Stadialism theory. *See* Marr, Nikolaj Jakovlevič
Stalin, Joseph, 116, *117*, 118, 161nn. 26, 30–31, 162n. 32
Steiner, George: *After Babel: Aspects of Meaning and Translation, 103*, 160nn. 2, 6
Stockwell, Robert, vii, 83
Structuralism, 32–33, 34–35, 36–39, 44, 71–72, 109, 113; in Czechoslovakia, 35, 37; in France, 36, 38; in Germany, 37, 38; in Great Britain, 38, 58–59; in Italy, 37, 38; in the Soviet Union, 38, 119–20; in the United States, 35–36, 38–41, 46–47, 51, 53, 61–62, 82–83, 154n. 8. *See also* Egalitarianism in linguistics
Studies in Linguistics (journal), 53
Sturtevant, Edgar, 42, 155n. 14
Stylistics, 8
Substandard languages. *See* Egalitarianism in linguistics
Summer Institute of Linguistics (SIL), 59–61, 157n. 51

Superstructural nature of language. *See* Sociological linguistics
Synchrony, 27–28, 31, 35, 143
Syntax, 9, 10–11, 33, 65–68, 73–74, 78
Systematicity of language, 6, 32, 35

Third World nations, languages of, 5, 59–61, 123–24
Torode, Brian: *The Material Word, 114*, 161n. 22
Trager, George, 42, 154n. 12; *Outline of Linguistic Analysis*, 53
Transcendental realities, 114
Transformational generative grammar. *See* Grammar, generative or transformational

Unconscious. *See* Linguistic changes and the unconscious
Universal grammar, 67–70, 74, 76–77, 93, 103, 144–45
Ural-Altaic languages, 56

Valian, Virginia, *147*, 163n. 14
Visual perception. *See* Cognition
Vocabulary, 136
Vološinov, V. N.: *Marxism and the Philosophy of Language*, 106–7, *109–10*, 160n. 8, 161nn. 10–13

War and linguistics. See Linguistic scholarship, government sponsorship of
Wellesley, marquess of, 57
Whorf, Benjamin L., 52, 110–*11*, 137, 161nn. 15–17
Williams, Raymond: *Marxism and Literature, 113–14*, 161nn. 20–21
Word (journal), 53
Word stress in English, 71
Worldview and language. *See* Sociological linguistics
Wycliffe Bible Translators. *See* Linguistic scholarship, church support of

Zvegincev, V. A., 120

YALE UNIVERSITY